SUCCESS PATHS BUSINESS SERIES

How to Sell Your Business Without a Broker

Ted Clifton

How to Sell Your Business Without a Broker
Ted Clifton
Paperback edition 978-1-77342-113-1
Ebook edition 978-1-77342-112-4

Published by PurpleSage Books LLC
www.TedClifton.com

Produced by IndieBookLauncher.com
www.IndieBookLauncher.com
Cover Design: Saul Bottcher
Interior Design and Typesetting: Saul Bottcher

The body text of this book is set in Adobe Caslon.

Contents

Introduction

This book is about selling your small/medium sized business without using the services of a business broker. It will give you the information and knowledge that you need to understand the process and methodology of selling a business.

The book has twelve chapters that address all the critical aspects of selling your business, telling you what steps are required and what you should do to accomplish your goal. As a bonus, it includes my ten-lesson course on How to Value a Small Business, along with a sample non-disclosure agreement and a sample due diligence list for stock transactions.

By reading this book, will you sell your business? Obviously, there is no way I can assure you of that. The variables involved in selling a business are extensive; beginning with what type of business it is, how much the owner wants for the business and on and on. What I am trying to do in this book is help you become familiar with the best approaches to reach the goal of selling your business. Your success will depend on you and your efforts.

My background is financial (CPA) with over 30 years' experience helping small/medium sized business owners sell their businesses—as an advisor/broker. I have written a book that will help you avoid hiring a broker, but my first advice would be to hire one. Yes, that's right, hire a business broker/representative. While fees may seem remarkably high, most businesses that are sold to someone other than family members are represented by a broker.

It takes a certain personality to comfortably represent oneself in this type of transaction. If you have that personality and have the knowledge contained in this book you can sell your business without a broker. But let me emphasize *it is not easy*.

Also, while I think it is possible to sell your own business with a strong commitment and extensive effort without a business broker, I *do not* think you can accomplish this without having adequate professional guidance. That includes at least an attorney and accountant. Depending on the size and complexity of the deal this may involve hiring other professionals. It is critical that you hire these people and have them involved in the total process.

Selling a business is a legal transaction that has little or none of the protections that exist for real estate and can create all kinds of contingent liabilities even after the deal has closed. You should find a business lawyer who has experience in the size deal you are contemplating and then take their advice. One caveat to that statement is to be leery of the attorney who wants to protect your interests so much, they create additional risk for the buyer and cause the buyer to back away from the deal. That attorney has protected your risks so well he has stopped you from selling your business. Each side has some risk in these deals, and you will need an attorney who understands the process and what risks are acceptable.

1
Is it Time to Sell?

This book examines the possibility of selling your business and the mechanics of getting that done. All businesses can be sold. The questions may be at what price and how long will it take? Some business owners will find it better to "liquidate" their assets and just close the doors. Many retail businesses will use that method to "exit" a business rather than take a deep discount on inventory to attract a buyer.

To understand your options, you should prepare an analysis that looks at the possible outcomes of selling your business (and the most common two methods that can accomplish that; stock sale or asset sale) and what you would anticipate as your bottom-line number after taxes and compare that with a liquidation scenario. The value of an operating business will almost always exceed the value of liquidation; but there are circumstances where you will need to know what the estimated outcome would be under several scenarios.

The exception to the operating business being worth more than a liquidation of the assets is when the business is losing money. Obviously, a business that is running in the red is not an attractive investment—unless the buyer can understand why the loses have occurred and how they can be fixed. As we will see in most things related to the purchase of a business the buyer is concerned with the future. The buyer will examine the past to understand the business; but what the buyer is buying is the future. So, under certain circumstances a buyer will pay for a losing business if it is clear that the future will be different. But those are unique and difficult deals to accomplish.

A key aspect in selling any business is the current owner's ability to "carry" a portion of the purchase price. If an owner is able and willing to carry a portion of the price, and especially if the owner is willing to subordinate that debt, it increases the chances of selling the business dramatically. This may seem obvious, but many business owners fight this reality by being unwilling to even consider any owner financing. This aspect will be discussed in more detail in the chapter "Structuring a Deal". The point here is that there are many aspects that will enter into a decision to sell.

When considering whether it is time to sell there are 5 key elements to examine:

- Are there buyers?
- Is your business trending up or down?
- Are you in a position to offer some owner financing?
- Is your business financially stable?
- Do you have a clear personal objective?

Are there buyers?

Probably seems like an obvious question, but many sellers have spent extraordinarily little time examining this key question. Small businesses may not have any idea where the buyer will come from except from the general public. This is not good. You should do research to try and identify buyers who might have an interest in your type of business. One of the first sources would be people in your industry. Many sellers are reluctant to approach people who may be or could become competitors. While it should be done with caution this is often the best source of potential buyers. If your business requires special licensing, skills or training then those groups become a good source for buyers. Do you have key employees or even ex-employees who might be interested in buying the business? Being able to compile a list of people, companies, groups, associations, contacts and prospects is a key to selling any business. If you cannot identify specific targets as potential buyers, you may want to rethink selling until you can identify those likely buyers.

Note: This book is about selling your business without a broker, but if you were going to use a broker, being able to identify possible buyers will help the broker focus advertising and improve the odds of actually selling your business.

Another approach is to market your business with targeted advertising. This often involves using on-line resources to advertise that the business is for sale. This can be done with limited information and no specific information identifying the business (a blind ad). This approach may generate some inquiries but remember that this approach will also generate some non-buyers who like to look at businesses. Qualifying these people is a major drawback to this approach. You should be ready to talk to some people you might consider "crazy" who would like to buy your business but have zero money to invest. And of course, any ad will generate some inquiries from brokers.

We will discuss later ways in which to market your business; but the most important aspect is to understand who the most likely buyer would be.

The size of your company will be a factor in determining who would buy your business.

Most national buyers will be looking for businesses doing $15M in revenue or greater depending on your industry, most financial buyers (private equity groups) are looking for substantial

EBITDA (earnings before interest, taxes, depreciation and amortization) and usually a fit with (add-on) to an existing portfolio company.

The hardest company to sell is a small company with a target buyer of the "general public". This almost never leads to success. You must narrow the search for a buyer down to attributes that you can identify and then go about searching (marketing) to those people who have those attributes.

> **Example.**
> *Type of business: Auto repair shop*
> *Revenue: $1.2M*
> *Profit before income taxes: $75K*
> *Owner's discretionary income: $155K*
> *Asking price: $425K*
> *Terms: $225K down, buyers note to seller $200K*
> *Value of tangible assets:*
> *—leasehold improvements $150K,*
> *—equipment/tools $100,*
> *—other assets $50K;*
> *Total assets $300K*
>
> *The owner of this business took an aggressive approach to marketing the business. He knew that the general public was not going to be the likely source of his buyer. He was a hands-on owner and fully expected to sell to someone much like himself.*
>
> *He put together a one-page summary of the business that highlighted the business in terms of type of work, specialty, future prospects, number of employees and summary financial data for the last 4 years. There was nothing in this one-page summary that would identify*

the specific business. He identified about 100 people/ organizations that he thought might represent someone who would be interested. This included his entire list of competitors in his general area and neighboring towns, suppliers, chamber of commerce's, a mechanic trade school located in a neighboring city, CPA offices in his area and others.

He also ran several blind ads in local newspapers and several on-line sources.

All of these efforts were directed to a new phone number he secured that accepted voice mail only and a new Gmail email account.

To supplement this effort, he also contacted personally over 50 friends, family and past associates and advised them that he was selling and planning on retiring. He asked these people if they knew of anyone who might be interested and if so to refer them to him directly.

The next step was to tell his employees. Like all business owners he was nervous about this step; but was gratified once he told his employees, how eager they were to learn more and assist in any way they could.

From this came 12 inquiries directed to the voice mail and Gmail account asking for additional information. Of these it appeared from the messages that about 5 had merit. The owner contacted those 5 and agreed to meet 3 who seemed the most interested.

There were also almost 8 inquires as a result of his calls to his personal list. Two of those turned out to be competitors who had also received the one-page summary. From the one-page summary there was 1 additional response. And there was interest expressed by 1 employee.

The results of his efforts were 22 inquiries and 6 who the owner felt were serious possibilities. Also, the owner received several phone calls from people who said that they had heard he was selling and wanted to wish him luck. There is no way to properly market a business and not have people know what you are doing—no matter how careful.

This owner did sell his business. After many months of discussion, he sold it to a partnership of one of his employees and a businessman who owned a supply business in another town. That partnership came about due to the owner's marketing approach since he brought these two together after talking to them individually. He ended up reducing the price some and taking an earn-out over 3 years if the business achieved certain revenue goals.

Asking that question "Are there buyers?" is one of the first steps in making the decision to sell. In order to achieve success, you must be able to put together a plan of action that will identify the most likely buyer (by attributes) and lay-out how that buyer will be found.

Is your business trending up or down?

Too often sellers will start to think about selling when their business is not doing well. Common sense tells us that is not the best time to sell. If you have read our course material (see Appendix) about valuing a business, you will know that value is based on the expected future financial performance of a business. If your business is trending down, you may have trouble finding a buyer and if you do find a buyer more than likely the buyer will want to pay a price based on continued down trends. While some businesses can be sold based upon a turn-around scenario—those businesses usually sell at "fire-sale" prices.

The best time to sell your business is when things are going well and there is optimism about the future. A buyer is buying the future so even though you may have had the best year ever last year it is what is anticipated in the future that the buyer is concerned about. So, you want to sell your business not at the top of its performance but slightly below. Of course, this can be very hard to predict. But to have the best chance of selling your business, time your sell for when the business is doing well and expected to continue for the feasible future.

As we know timing in life is a significant aspect of success. When selling a business—timing is everything. Buyers will look at historical numbers to help them estimate the value of the business, but it is trends that really drive buyer interest and higher values. As has been said several times the buyer is buying the future—the past is only meaningful in assisting the buyer in "guessing" at the future.

Sellers who have not purchased a business themselves sometimes will not appreciate the level of risk a buyer is taking. The selling business could have a tremendous track record for the last 5 years but for reasons not controlled by the owner could fall flat on its face in the 6th year. It happens.

It is trends that build the confidence in a buyer. If the business is trending down most buyers will just walk away from any deal, unless it is a fire-sale bargain; no matter what historical numbers have been.

Unless health or other reasons force a sale, the seller should wait to sell the business until there are positive trends and a bright future. Of course, sometimes that cannot work. My approach with negative trends has always been to be candid with the buyer and lay-out a detailed plan on how the business could turn-around. That might keep a buyer interested but the price will be much lower.

Owners of businesses should plan the sale of their business to maximize value based on their anticipation of positive growth trends for the short-term and long-term.

Are you in a position to offer some owner financing?

As a seller if you can offer owner financing you improve the odds of selling. The more you can (and are willing) to do the more your chances of selling, and at your price, will increase. Conversely if you have to have all cash you limit your chances of selling. Most small businesses do not have the collateral base or cash flow to support borrowing a high percentage of the asking price. As a result, you are asking the buyer to invest substantial cash to do the deal. While some buyers may be in a position to do that most will not have the cash available to accomplish the deal. There are many issues about owner financing such as the risk of collecting and proper legal protection and collateral. A seller needs to be very cautious and do extensive due diligence before agreeing to any type of owner financing; but as a seller, if you can provide this financing, you improve the odds of selling your business—dramatically.

Is your business financially stable?

Much like the trend question but in a different perspective. If your business is on the verge of bankruptcy your chances of selling are slim. Even if your business is not on the verge of bankruptcy but is operating at a loss you may not be able to survive long enough to sell. Most sellers of businesses in trouble will not make the price/terms concessions they need to make in order to sell their business. Always remember you are selling the future, so if your business is losing now you are asking a buyer to take a substantial risk that it will continue to lose at the current, or worse, rate in the future. To take that risk requires incentives in the form of a low price and maybe good terms. In most cases the owner of a financially unstable business will not be able to find a buyer and negotiate a deal before it is too late. This is especially true with small businesses that usually do not have access to resources to keep the doors open while looking for a buyer.

Do you have a clear personal objective?

Most small business sellers want to say to a potential buyer that they do not care whether they sell or not. If the business doesn't sell, they will just keep running it. This is because they don't want the buyer to think they are in financial trouble and have to sell. However, this is completely wrong. If you are selling your business, it should be because you have a clear objective that involves selling. That might be retirement, boredom, health reasons, other business interests, want to go play and spend money—whatever it is; it should include selling the business. When you tell the buyer that you have clear personal plans that involve selling the business and doing something else you are telling the buyer that you are a serious seller, and he is not wasting his time looking at your business. If you do not have a clear objective about selling your business and what you are going to do after you have sold, you will not be an effective seller of your business. The best sellers of businesses are the owners who have a clear vision of where they will be after the sell and concentrate their efforts into accomplishing that objective.

After you have examined those five areas you should have a much better idea on whether this is a good time to sell or not. In many cases a close examination of your business and you will reveal that it is not a good time to sell. The best thing to do at that point is to establish an objective of selling your business in the future and began the work to put your business in a better position by that time.

2
How to Price your Business

After you have decided to sell your business one of the first questions is how much is it worth? There are many ways to approach this question, including not answering the question at all. You could put your business on the market without a price and see it you got an offer. In a very theoretical sense that offer could be the market value (not likely). That is not what we would recommend. But determining the value of your business is not a simple process. You can estimate the value yourself or you can hire a valuator (business appraiser). As a bonus to this book included in the appendix is a step-by-step process detailing and explaining how to value a privately owned small business. There are 10 lessons written by me that should help you understand how to value your business.

Your decision on whether to hire someone to do a valuation would depend on the size and complexity of your business. Many small businesses can be valued using some of the techniques we will discuss later with reasonable accuracy and therefore it would not make sense to hire a valuator. On the other hand, many business owners would benefit from a valuation, both in knowing a professional opinion of value and in the knowledge gained from the information used to compile that value. A valuation report can be a useful tool in the marketing of your business.

One of the biggest keys in understanding value is to remember that a buyer is buying the future not the past. The value of your business is based on the future benefit it can bring its owner. Past performance is used as a benchmark of what a business will do in the future—but always keep in mind that it is the future of your business that you are selling.

Below are excerpts from *How to Value a Small Business*, which is included later in this book as a 2-in-1 bonus:

> *The value of any business is actually a very simple concept. But while simple in theory it is often difficult to actually determine. Value is based on the ability of a business to generate a stream of funds into the future. Or in other words how profitable will this business be in the years ahead.*
>
> *If you could predict with complete accuracy the future profits (or cash flow) of a business, you could easily determine its value. By knowing the future income stream, the value would be based on the investors (buyers) desired return as compared to other investment alternatives. So, if a business could generate $100,000 per year return to its owner without the owner's active involvement and with some reasonable assurance that this would occur every year; the buyer might say the business was worth $1,250,000 which would be an 8% return on his investment. Simple.*
>
> *Now the problem; nobody knows the future. And with businesses you better believe you do not know the future. You could have a company with a consistent track record of increased profits for the last twenty years, and in the twenty-first year lose money! The reasons could be management, your product is suddenly obsolete, the global economy, the national economy, the local economy, the weather, the stars; you name it, and it can affect business.*

So, if determining the value of a business is based on predicting the future, you probably should go see a physic rather than a business consultant, right? Well maybe! The answer you get could be as useful. However, there are ways of determining a "good guess" at the future performance of a business, the past. Keeping in mind the example above of the company with a consistent twenty-year profitable track record and then losing in the twenty-first; nevertheless, in most cases the past is a very good indicator of the future. A company that has been in business twenty years is going to be a lot easier to forecast into the future than one that has been in business only a few years.

The quality and quantity of historical information enters into an analysis that determines the "risk" associated with the future of a business. The elements that determine risk are as numerous as the elements that effect a business performance; the global to local economies, competition, management stability, management skills, capital requirements, cost of capital, product/service stability, customer demographics, supplier's stability, location of the business and on and on.

Therefore, in the simplest of terms a business is worth its ability to generate future profits (or cash flow) modified by a risk factor, which incorporates all elements of risk associated with predicting and producing those future profits. Easy to say, hard to calculate.

Shannon P. Pratt, a widely recognized valuation authority, describes this theory and its complications more elegantly:

A generally accepted theoretical structure underlies the process of valuing a business interest. In theory, the value of an interest in a business depends on the future benefits that will accrue to it, with the value of the future benefits discounted back to a present value at some appropriate discount (capitalization) rate. Thus, the theoretically correct approach is to project the future benefits (usually earnings, cash flow, or dividends) and discount the projected stream back to a present value.

However, while there is general acceptance of a theoretical framework for business valuation, translating it into practice in an uncertain world poses one of the most complex challenges of economic and financial theory and practice.[1]

Some of this may sound like gobbledygook, but if you are a seller or a buyer of a business it is important to understand the concepts of value. The value of your business may be determined by an industry specific rule-of-thumb or many other methods that attempt to simplify the basics described above into something that is easier to calculate and understand. But it will be based on the basic principle of future benefits modified by a risk factor. Understanding this puts you in a better position to make a deal that works for you.

As we have recently seen in some of the more bizarre examples with .com public companies, value is based on a

---

1   Shannon P. Pratt, *Valuing a Business, The Analysis and Appraisal of Closely Held Companies*, Second Edition (Dow Jones-Irwin, 1981 and 1989), p. 35

perception of the future. While the more dramatic examples of this tend to occur in publicly traded companies where individual investors may not be risking a large portion of their personal wealth, this is still a valid concept with privately held businesses. A business is worth what a "buyer/investor" perceives as future reward associated with the business. A business that has a unique concept or product will have a much higher "perceived" value to investor/buyers than a ho-hum business model.

The challenge to the valuator is to be able to understand and translate "sizzle" into value without overstating the future potential of an unproven business. The easiest business to value is one with a proven, stable track record; the hardest is one with great (but unproven) potential.

Many businesses can be valued using simple formulas unique to their industry; these are called rules-of-thumb. These are important numbers to know, even though they can be wrong. If your industry has a rule-of-thumb, then that is the first value you need to know. These can be simple formulas such as 1 times annual revenue, or 70% of annual revenue, or 4 times earnings before interest and taxes (EBIT), or 4 times earnings before interest, taxes, depreciation and amortization (EBITDA), or 1.5 times owner's discretionary income or cash flow, or X times number of rooms, or X times number of gallons sold and on and on. Almost every business will have a rule-of-thumb that is common knowledge within that industry.

These rules change as the marketplace changes, but they are slow to change and can represent outdated or inaccurate thinking. These rules come about as averages on deals that have been done, so they do somewhat reflect the market. But they tend to filter out the more complicated aspects of deals, such as terms, post-closing adjustments, performance guarantees and other factors that are not easy to translate into a common formula. Another key area to remember regarding these rules is that no one is monitoring this information to ensure that it is accurate. Transaction numbers can end up in the marketplaces that are completely inaccurate. This can be because the deal was not a simple all cash transaction easy to interpret; to the fact that the seller or buyer chose to lie about what the deal was. There is no government body or anybody else gathering this information and making sure it is correct. Rules-of-thumb should be used but used with caution.

There are good sources for rule-of-thumb information. That includes books written on the subject, which will list the rule-of-thumb for many different types of businesses. The best source often will be a trade association within your industry. If the trade association does not have an article or other material available discussing valuations within your industry you can request that they ask their members for input.

An area that will affect determining the value of your business will be restating or recasting your financial statements. The owner of a small closely held business has many "opportunities" to affect the financial performance of his or her business. To understand value, it is imperative that the financial data and operational data be examined to recognize adjustments that need to be made. Sometimes this is called "normalizing" earnings. To adjust the actual financial data to reflect the operation without the "unusual" items that might affect a particular period.

This is an area of much confusion and disagreement. Often a seller of a business will identify one-time operational issues that have had a negative impact on the business and want them adjusted back into the profit mix. A buyer will say that those so-called one-time expenditures are really just a normal cost of business and should be deducted to determine profits. This can create a wide difference of opinion as to what "normalized earnings" actually should be. This process of recasting financial statements is a major element in determining value of most closely held small businesses.

There are many approaches to determining value used by valuators. The most typical approaches are:

- Asset-based Methods.
- Capitalization of Earnings Method.
- Multiple of Discretionary Earnings Method.
- Rules of Thumb
- Excess Earnings Method.
- Discounted Future Earnings Method.

Each of these approaches is exampled in our 10 lessons on "How to Determine the Value of Your Business". For this book we will discuss the Rules of Thumb (above) and the Multiple of Discretionary Earnings Method. The reason I am limiting our discussion to these two methods is due to the fact they are fairly simple to use and there is market data available without much effort to support both methods.

The Multiple of Discretionary Earnings Method is based upon owner's discretionary income (or cash flow). The reason this measure and the market driven data supporting this as a basis of valuation came about is quite simple. Data from most small businesses is heavily skewed by owner's compensation. It is either too high or too low. In most cases it involves benefits that would not be afforded the average manager. As a result, most measures did not make sense unless you made adjustments for owner's comp and benefits. Therefore, why not just use the number before any of the owner's consideration is deducted which is called owner's discretionary income.

Plus, much of the decision about buying small businesses is based more on what you can take out as opposed to a more sophisticated return on investment analysis. Someone might think in terms of valuing a business based on the income they think they can make. So that person could decide that they would pay $300,000 for a business if they could make a $60,000 income for themselves. On the surface that might look like a 20% return, but if the owner will work in the business and he values his worth (as employee/manager) at $60,000; he is not making anything for his $300,000 investment. This would not seem to be a good deal; but buyers will value a business based on a lot of other factors besides income.

The more you learn about valuing a business the more likely you will hire a professional to determine the value. You can guess, you can use the market-based short-cuts but to know for sure you will have to spend some money and hired someone who has the expertise to establish value.

Risk is what drives value more than anything else. So even if you could "forecast" stabilized earnings (EBITDA or some other measure of benefit) you would still have to estimate risk. Each industry will have its own set of risks: for example, a restaurant will have a different risk profile than a manufacturing company. And calculating risk is where the value of a professional estimator comes into play. Taking an example; let us say we have $1M of stabilized earnings (EBITDA) from two different businesses— one is a very stable business with long-term history, professional management that will stay in place, excellent customer relations, revenues based on long-term binding contracts and the other one with a very short term erratic history, no key employees to replace the seller after the transaction, most of the business revenue from only one volatile customer and revenue based on short-term contracts which are bid every year.

The first business after analysis might have a risk factor (capitalization rate) of 18% while the second business could be 45%. The value of the first business would be $5.5M while the value of the second business would be $2.2M—dramatically different. And the surprising aspect is that they could both be in the same industry. But they have very different risk elements. Because they are in the same industry the short-cut methods (such as a multiple) would be the same. So, an industry norm of 4 times EBITDA would mean both businesses are worth $4M. The first business would be undervalued by $1.5M and the second business would be overvalued by $1.8M.

The above example may be extreme but, in my experience, I have seen values for business in the same industry with similar financial results that would vary by that amount because of risk elements. Understanding risk is what is driving the buyer—all of their analysis and due diligence is about trying to quantify risk; and it can have a huge impact on value.

Goodwill: what is it? When we are talking about value based on looking at cash flow or some other financial benefit to the owner we are obviously talking about value in excess of the assets of the business. The difference in value is goodwill. That represents the value associated with the business's earnings power over and above a minimal financial return on assets. I have often heard people refer to goodwill as "blue sky". More or less implying it is a made-up number with no meaning. That is not true. Goodwill is the accounting term applied to the difference in asset value and economic value of a business.

Think of a business with $500K in assets that generates $200K economic benefit to the owner and a business with $1M in assets that generates zero benefit to the owner. On an asset basis the second business could be worth $1M (but isn't) while on an economic basis the first business could be worth $650K. The difference between $500K asset value and $650K economic value is goodwill. If it was me I would rather have $150K in goodwill and own the first business as opposed to no goodwill and own the second one making no money.

Goodwill can often come about because of the nature of the business. A business (such as an engineering firm) that relies on human assets not physical assets will often have goodwill. This happens because we do not assign a dollar amount for human assets and place that amount on the balance sheet. Often service type business will have low asset ratios to their value but represent great business opportunities.

Once you can understand that what you are buying is the benefit generated by assets and not the assets themselves you start to see goodwill as a good thing not something bad. The value of a business is much more tied up in its reputation, history, collective knowledge and experience of its employees, customer relations, supplier relations and more as opposed to physical assets.

Rules-of-thumb are shorthand versions of more complex valuation models. Each industry will have its own quick and easy valuation formulas. There is nothing wrong with this approach as long as you understand it can be completely wrong.

Businesses are often valued based on a multiple of something. 1.5 times annual revenue, 3 times owners' discretionary income, or even x dollars for each active customer. These simplified formulas are based on real transaction but do not allow for any variances between one company and another. Even in the same industries and relatively the same size companies can be very different in what they are worth. Obvious factors can be the number of customers. Say two companies making a million in profits a year; one has one customer and the other has twenty more or less equal customers—are they worth the same amount?

Obviously one of those companies has much greater risk with the future than the other. That risk in any thoughtful analysis will value those companies very differently. A one size fits all formula does not do that.

This is an area where if you are not comfortable with the more complex methods of establishing value you should seek some assistance.

3

Prepare Your Business for Others to See

A buyer of a business is usually making a very important decision about his or her future. This decision might be the biggest financial decision they will ever make. The buyer, understandably, is very concerned about the risks associated with this decision. Much of this concern is trying to predict the future as it relates to the business.

Risk of failure and the analysis of that risk is what will determine whether a buyer will go forward with a deal. A buyer has several ways of trying to understand and limit their risk associated with buying a particular business.

These areas break down into 3 broad categories:

- **Documentation.** This includes financial statements, supporting financial data, leases, operating procedures, customer lists, employee contracts/agreements, patents, copyrights, legal documents, payroll records, employee records and on and on. Depending on the size of the deal this can quite literally be a mountain of paper.
- **Business assets.** This includes facilities, furniture fixtures and equipment, inventory and all tangible assets, along with accounts receivables, logos and all intangible assets.
- **Intuition.** This is where buyers get good or bad feelings about a business. This can be based on the appearance of the business, housekeeping or the attitude of the seller. All very subjective.

28

Reviewing all documentation before buying a business is obvious. Often this review will be called due diligence. Which is to say; the buyer is making sure that he or she understands what they are buying, and the information is accurate and reliable. As a seller the better prepared you are for this to happen the more likely that you will have a smooth transaction.

When I have functioned as a broker, one of the first things I tell sellers is; be prepared to answer a lot of "stupid" questions and provide a lot of documents based upon "stupid" requests. Of course, a lot of the questions and requests for documents are not "stupid". But most sellers start to lose patience with buyers who seem to have an unending need for just a little bit more information. It is important to understand that what the buyer is doing (usually unknowingly) is trying to find something that he is not sure what it is. In other words, he may not really care about last year's workman's comp insurance premium, but he picked that arbitrarily to see if it was a problem to provide. Also, buyers can make unreasonable requests to see if a seller is willing to provide the information. As a seller it is important to remember that buyers are very suspicious of the accuracy of the information that they have been given. In larger deals a buyer will hire an outside consultant or CPA to do much of this due diligence and then rely upon their report for assurance.

To prepare your company for these "inspections" you should do your own due diligence prior to any requests from buyers. Look at the conditions of your financial statements, gather all necessary supporting documents, and organize your data and information so it is easily accessible. This pre-due diligence can have a tremendous impact on the salability of your business and can pinpoint areas that need attention before the buyer sees them. There are due diligence checklists available in many books and from many trade associations that can help you identify the areas that a typical buyer will ask to see. Use this checklist to review where your company is and prepare for outside visitors. (Due diligence sample list included in Appendix)

This can amount to a lot of work before you even have a buyer interested in your business. But it is an effort that will pay off; both in the ease and speed that you will be able to respond to questions and requests, but also in the perception the buyer will have of your business. As we will mention in a minute intuition plays an important role in evaluating how risky a business deal is and having good information readily available and organized helps to create a positive intuitive feeling about the business.

The business assets are obviously the most tangible aspect of your business. Before you talk to a buyer you should have taken a complete inventory of those assets and made sure that your documentation and what actually exist agree. Besides making sure that you have 3 gizmos if that is what you are supposed to have; you should spend some time making the gizmos look as good as possible. Pride in your business will sell your business better than any other attribute. Your pride cannot be based on "lip-service" or it will backfire. I have set in meetings where a seller will talk about how proud he is of his business and what a difficult decision it was for him to decide to sell his "baby"; and then you go on a tour and everything looks like it has not been cleaned in months, there is trash everywhere, the equipment is obviously run-down and not maintained—immediately the buyer logs everything else this seller says into the "not sure he is telling the truth category".

You should also look at any underutilized or obsolete assets. If you have inventory that is not "marketable" it should be disposed of—even at a loss. Assets that are not being utilized can actually lesson the value of the business. A buyer wants good assets that are being utilized in the business—generating a return on the value of those assets. While excess equipment may seem acceptable to you, most likely a buyer will see additional insurance cost and storage/maintenance cost—not anything of value.

Owners of businesses can become enamored with their physical assets and hold on to them without consideration of the cost involved. This of course is not an issue if you are going to liquidate the business for the asset value—but if you are trying to maximize value based on earnings or cash flow, *excess* equipment has no value and as mentioned can have negative value. The best course of action is to prepare your business by selling excess equipment and other assets.

I am not saying a business has to look brand spanking new to sell—that is obviously not true; but it should look like the owner cares about the condition of the equipment, signs, plant—even employees if he wants to get the best price. If you are putting your business on the market at the rock-bottom fire-sale price, then you do not need to worry about housekeeping or equipment maintenance; but otherwise, you better give it some attention in advance. I have seen situations where a few hundred dollars in paint has made all of the difference in a several hundred thousand of dollars' deal.

Those are the physical assets but don't forget the other assets of the company. Make sure accounts receivable are in good shape, have your latest advertising material available—look at all aspect of your company's "assets" and make sure they are presentable.

Preparing your business for someone to examine requires a lot of hard work. It also takes some time and commitment to get it done. It will pay off. Business decisions are made by people (not number crunching machines) and those people are affected by intuitive feelings of comfort. Many deals do not happen because buyers develop uncomfortable "feelings" about a particular deal. That is based on the empirical evidence that they gather as they go about the review and inspection of the business. That is from the condition of the documents to general feelings during a site visit. If the buyer gets good "feelings" the chances improve dramatically for the deal to happen. I am not saying the numbers don't matter; but if you have two competing deals with identical earnings and perception of future performance but one has good documentation and appearance which one is going to happen?

A seller will improve their odds of selling their business greatly by doing some basic review and clean-up items before they have a buyer look at their business. This process of performing your own due diligence on your business will also prepare you to sell your business easier and faster if for no other reason than that you are prepared to address questions and deliver documents.

Think of selling your business as making the biggest and most important sales presentation you have ever made. Be prepared and you will do a much better job of presenting your business in the best light possible.

4
Normalized Earnings and Adjusted EBITDA

Most small businesses and many middle size companies are run solely for the benefit of one or a couple of owners (or the owner's family). As a result, there are often decisions made on the basis of owner benefit not necessarily what is best for the actual business. I have seen businesses that will have a relative on the payroll who does little (or nothing) beneficial to the business. An owner may decide to spend extra money and have a company car that is a luxury car—not necessary for the business. Owner's salaries can far exceed what a "normal" business of the same size and industry might pay. These sorts of expenditures can have a significant impact on the financial earnings of the company. As a result, the actual earnings capacity of the business is understated by these "discretionary" expenses.

Also, a business can have unusual expenses in any one period that would not be expected to occur in the future. This could be the result of accidents, theft, unusual lawsuits, re-organizations, strikes and many other things that can occur on an infrequent basis. These expenditures can be classified as "one-time" costs.

Another area that is a little bit greyer are items that are expensed for the purpose of reducing income taxes that could be treated in a different manner if taxes were not a consideration. The most common of these is expensing equipment costs and repair and maintenance that could be capitalized. This can have significant impact on value if the valuation model is using EBITDA (earnings before interest, taxes, depreciation and amortization) as base earnings.

It is very important that you evaluate these areas and develop detail information on these types of expenditures. The impact on value can be significant. Some buyers will be most comfortable with these types of adjustments; some buyers will balk at this and feel that the seller is just "messing" with the numbers.

But the theory on why there should be restatement or adjustment of the financial numbers is sound. The buyer is looking for normalized earnings that reflect the true financial performance of the business. The fact that the owner chooses to pay his brother a salary for doing nothing will not impact the future earnings of the business under a different owner.

The impact of these adjustments is directly related to value. This is discussed in greater detail in the appendix: 10 Lessons on How to Value a Small Business. But in essence anything that adds to the bottom line (as these adjustments will) will increase the value of the business. A professional evaluator will add back these expenses to arrive at estimated "normalized" earnings as a basis for some of their financial models. You should also do that.

The better support documentation you have for these adjustments the easier it is for the buyer to accept that they are legitimate amounts that need to be considered. To reach the maximum value for the business you will have to "addback" these items—unless of course your business is very unusual and has none of these types of adjustments.

The best approach to have proper support and accurate information is to start tracking these types of expenditures on an on-going basis. This will also assist you in measuring the true performance of the business. Just keep a spreadsheet with these items and possibly a file with documentation.

Most of these types of expenditures are tax deductible so you are not "cheating" on your taxes. The fact that you choose to have a life insurance policy on yourself paid for by the business or drive an expensive car or even pay your brother-in-law twice what he is worth is your business decision and tax deductible (as long as it meets the IRS guidelines and rules for business expenses). Same with expenses of R&M or equipment as opposed to expensing—there is leeway in the IRS rules you can interpret in different ways—usually the most important aspect is to be consistent.

Some sellers will go to extremes with these "addbacks" and try to include bad business results as adjustments. Such as a poor manager who made mistakes that cost the company money. Almost no buyers will accept operational matters as one-time events or any type of addback. If you just dump a bunch of stuff into addbacks and wait and see what sticks you run the risk of having the buyer reject all of your addbacks out of hand because of the "strange" ones. I recommend that you keep addbacks to a minimum and only use the ones that are acceptable (easy to understand) and non-operational issues. These usually are obvious, such as the ones that have been mentioned and will not cause a buyer to flinch.

5
Confidential Information Memorandum

In most deals handled by professional representatives there are two key documents that are used to communicate with potential buyers. One is the "blind" summary (usually one or two pages) that offers a brief narrative and summary financial information without disclosing any information or data that would identify the business; the second is the Confidential Information Memorandum (CIM), which used to be referred to as an offering memorandum or selling memorandum.

The summary as we will discuss later is the marketing tool that can be sent (email mostly) to potential prospects to test their interest level. This is sent without having any confidentiality agreements in place (NDA's) that is why it must be done in a way where the business cannot be identified. Once a party expresses some interest and has signed an NDA—they are sent the CIM.

As the owner of the business representing yourself you can handle this in any manner that is comfortable to you. There are no rules here. The most important thing to keep in mind is that the first stage of contact will almost always be before NDA's are signed (unless you have already identified the buyer and there is not going to be a search for a buyer) and as a result they need to be structured in a way that conveys enough info/data to create interest but does not disclose anything that would be considered confidential including the identity of the business.

The sections of the CIM most likely would include:

- Statement of use related to confidentiality.
- Summary sheet prepared for email.
- Executive summary describing the business.
- Narrative describing the business in greater detail.
    - Industry
    - Business services/products
    - Markets
    - Facilities
    - Employees (organizational chart)
    - Equipment/Assets
    - Customers
    - Competitors
    - All material that would be important for a buyer to make an informed decision.
- Financial
    - Brief narrative regarding financial performance.
    - Historical information.
    - Current operational data.
    - Future Prospects.
    - Projections.
    - Historical adjusted Financials/EBITDA.
- Summary.
- Attachments can include financial statements, tax returns, bios on key management members, equipment lists, customer/market detail and more.

Smaller deals would generally have smaller packages of information and larger deals will be extensive.

As a broker/representative I have always recommended to my clients that they include projections/forecasts in with this information. Some sellers are reluctant. This is only an estimate or your best guess at where the business is headed. Larger companies will have this data readily available. For the smaller business owner this may feel like a burden to prepare; but it will help the buyer see where you think the business is headed. Make it reasonable and believable—but be aggressive about your positive attitude about the future. Remember that is what the buyer is buying, the future financial results.

6
Marketing Your Business

Many business owners think that the only challenge in selling their business is how to market the business. While marketing is critical it is only part of the job. Some sellers who think that marketing is the complete key; will nevertheless limit marketing efforts due to confidentiality concerns.

The best way to market your business for sale is like all marketing—let as many people know as possible. You cannot sell your business if you do not let people know that it is for sale. Many business owners do not want their employees to know, or their banker, or their suppliers, or their competitors and on and on. There are legitimate concerns about confidentiality—but my experience suggests that there is a direct correlation between concerns for secrecy and being able to successfully sell your business. If you can only let selected people know your business is for sale and then restrict severely what they can know; your chances of selling that business decrease dramatically.

The best approach to marketing your business and maintaining confidentiality as required for your circumstances is to put together a marketing plan. You should examine every aspect of that plan. How to advertise? What to say in your ads? How do prospects respond—phone, email, mail? Who handles the responses? Will there be a package of data readily available? Who gets a confidentiality agreement signed? The marketing plan should address these issues and more prior to starting the process of selling the business. In many cases putting together the plan shows the weakness in keeping the sale secret. You may need the assistance of your employees to conduct a successful marketing campaign to sell the business. You may need assistance from your suppliers or your banker or others to complete a transaction.

Business owners are reluctant to take an aggressive open approach to marketing their businesses because they feel it will have a negative impact on the business itself. There may be cases where that is true. In most cases that is not true. I recommend that a business owner take significant time to analyze whether they want to sell and once they decide that they do, they should approach the process with a clear understanding that their new objective in their business is to sell. That means that you understand and anticipate the negative reactions. You deal with them in advance of any surprises.

Your marketing plan should consist of the following:

- Identify the likely prospects.
- How is the best way to contact these prospects?
- Prepare a one-page summary of your business.
- Prepare a selling memorandum describing your business in detail.
- Decide who will respond to inquiries and how.
- Prepare a confidentiality agreement (or non-disclosure agreement) for prospects to sign.
- Prepare a list of typical questions and responses from a prospect about your business.
- Prepare a list of questions you would like answered by a prospect before you divulge additional information.
- Make sure that you have access to a good attorney, CPA (accountant) and financial planner.

How to identify likely prospects? If there is one key area to selling your business this is it. If you come to the conclusion that the only way you can characterize the likely buyer for your business is someone who has the money—you could be in trouble. While there are marketing approaches to the general public (business opportunity ads), marketing works best when you can identify you prospects and target your advertising.

As we briefly said in chapter one, the most likely prospects are often competitors, employees, ex-employees, suppliers or synergistic industries. If there are special skills required or licensing this can sometimes help target buyers. Even though you may decide not to market to a particular group for confidentiality reasons you should identify all groups that might represent likely buyers. This of course may be the general public, but what you would be after is a detailed list of the type of buyers who would be most likely to buy a business in your industry, or location, or size of business— any characteristic that can be used to target the prospects.

With this information you can now decide how best to contact these prospects. This could be phone calls, or ads in trade association papers, ads in specialty magazines or papers, direct mail to selected groups or networking with suppliers. *If people do not know your business is for sale you will not sell your business!* To sell your business without a broker requires that *you* make contact with the prospective buyers in some manner.

Another way to think about this process is to think of the typical buyer of a small business. Most typically this is an individual (or a small group of two to three partners) with a very specific interest and defined target date to complete the deal. The most typical buyer is not someone who has looked for a business to buy for a long period of time but is someone who through circumstances is in a position to finance a business purchase and is motivated to buy, now. These are not people who will sit around waiting on an ad to appear in the paper describing the type of business they want to purchase. They are pro-active and are taking steps to identify likely prospects that fit their criteria.

The person who waits for the ads in the paper is a shopper. This person has looked at 10's to 100's of possible businesses to buy and has yet to find the deal that works. This person will never, *never* find the deal that works. They just waste your time and create a lot of frustration. This type of person alone may be reason enough not to run general business opportunity ads.

But the real buyer is searching and is eager to make a deal. He will contact trade associations in the industries he is interested in, he will contact suppliers of the industries he is interest in, he will contact CPA's, bankers, attorneys and he will contact business brokers. This person will be looking in all of the ways they can think of—you need to put yourself in their path.

Understanding the buyer emphasizes the number one thing a seller should do and that is networking. You need to contact everyone (you are willing to) and tell him or her about this wonderful (once in a lifetime) opportunity that exists. The more people you contact and encourage them to contact others the more people will become aware that your business is for sale.

That is my recommended approach. Not everybody wants to do that. For reasons that can be valid it is not in the best interest of the company to let anyone know that the business is for sale. Obviously, you have to let someone know. While this approach can be very limiting to successfully closing a deal there are approaches that can be done while limiting the number of people who are aware that the business is for sale.

Many times, business owners will end up with a business broker for this very reason. The broker will assure them that all advertising and marketing will done in such a manner that no one will know who the company is until they have signed confidentiality agreements and have been determined to be a qualified buyer. This may be a very valid reason to use a broker.

What is a one-page summary of the business? This is brief information about your business in a short narrative along with summary financial data. Usually, the financial data is for 3 to 5 years of revenue, gross margin, profits and EBITDA. This is often adjusted EBITDA which is adding back items that are non-recurring or non-operational items.

What is a selling memorandum (or Confidential Information Memorandum [CIM])? This is the document along with attachments you would provide to a potential buyer after they have signed an NDA that will tell them the story of your business and provide sufficient financial data that can determine their level of interest and possibly develop a value for your business.

There are many creative ways to convey information. The use of photos, video, web sites, graphics/charts; all can add to the presentation quality of your material. I recommend being creative and aggressive with your presentation materials. However, keep in mind that what drives most deals (at least at the beginning) is well presented financial data. Most buyers will examine the initial financial data more than anything else to determine if they are interested in pursuing the deal.

I think the overall quality of the presentation materials can add to the "good feelings" a buyer has about the opportunity—and that is important. On the other hand, do not spend excessive amounts or overly worry about these materials; the buyer will not buy your business just because you have the most professional presentation materials.

7
How to Protect Confidential Information

A parallel of selling your business would be a doctor treating a patient—*"first do no harm"*. If you do not sell your business, you want to make sure that the process of marketing the business and disclosing information does not cause you economic harm. In my experience this is one of the areas where hiring a broker can be most beneficial. They have the expertise to test the market for buyers without divulging confidential materials.

But no matter who is handling the sale eventually *all* information related to the business will have to be disclosed. You cannot sell a business and not disclose all information that the buyer feels are needed to fully understand and evaluate the business. This, of course, can be customer information, bidding information, company formulas, employee information, contractual information and more. This can be very uncomfortable for the seller.

I have had sellers tell me they will not disclose certain information until they have a binding commitment from the buyer. There is no information about a business that a buyer will not want to see before there is a binding commitment. This causes many deals to fall through.

Part of the method to make this acceptable to the seller to provide this information is based on legal documents that both parties agree to regarding confidentiality. This is very important, and we will discuss in more detail later. My experience is that the most important aspect of making a deal happen is trust. Some of the most important meetings/phone calls are at the very beginning when a seller and buyer meet. If they can establish a sense of trust and believe all parties are acting in good faith the likelihood of a deal happening increase significantly. If for some reason one side or the other comes away from these initial discussions with a "feeling" of mistrust—no number of legal documents will offset the distrust and no deal will happen.

When functioning as a broker it was often my practice not to attend these first meetings between buyer and seller. If they could not meet and talk and get to know one another a deal was most likely not going to happen anyway. Having a third party (lawyer, broker, and accountant) would just get in the way of the deciding parties establishing whether they can work together and make something happen.

The advice I have given sellers is if it feels uncomfortable just walk away. This can be tough to do but almost always you are walking away from something that was not going to occur anyway.

The hardest deal to complete is between competitors. In many cases the most likely buyer for a business is someone already in that business. Sharing confidential information with a competitor can be almost impossible for some owners. Remember that the majority of what you might consider confidential information is probably available to someone if they really wanted it. Customers, employee lists, bidding practices, contract terms can almost always be determined by a competitor if they so desire. Very little business dealings are done in secret. Thinking about what is really confidential and what might potentially cause the company harm if known helps to determine how you manage information and data.

If your business has "secret" information/formulas or business practices that you have determined would be harmful if divulged and used by someone against your company—then you would need to take an extra step and establish stricter non-disclosure agreements for those specific secrets. With extremely sensitive information you should hire a lawyer to draft the appropriate NDA that would offer the maximum legal protection and remedies for those specific concerns.

However, if the information is more general in nature and while confidential, knowing it would not create over whelming financial risk for the seller, a more standard NDA would be adequate.

The most important aspect of this chapter is that you cannot sell a business without disclosing confidential information. If you think you can you are mistaken. Lawyers and the legal protection they can create in documents can be helpful; but the best protection is to deal with people you trust. Or said another way if you know your competitor is a crook and would go to any lengths to cause you harm; you exclude that person from any consideration.

While it is not part of the discussion on legal protection for confidential information one aspect of the sale of the business is the reluctance of the seller to let anyone know they are considering selling. Obviously, this is due to the concern that a competitor will use that knowledge to undermine relationships with customers or suppliers, or that employees will feel unsecure about their jobs or lessen performance standards. These are legitimate concerns. My advice has always been the same, let everyone know you are considering selling the business.

I believe this is harder to do with small business because the owners are so self-identified with their businesses. But if your goal is to sell your business and you have taken all of the analytical steps described before to determine that you have a viable business that should sell at the price you desire then you should move forward to achieve that objective. And you cannot achieve that objective without letting people know.

Anyone who thinks they can sell a business in a vacuum has not tried it, because it will not work. The ideal situation would be to let everyone who could possibly be interested (or know someone who could possibly be interested) in buying the business know that it is for sale. Like most things in business this is about risk vs reward.

The basic legal document to protect confidential information is a Non-Disclosure Agreement (NDA) or sometimes called a Confidentiality Agreement (CA). These documents are doing the same thing—laying out what confidential data/information is and that the receiving party will not disclose this information outside of the process of evaluating the business for purchase. Also remedies for breach are listed.

There are many free sources for these types of agreements and the various elements are most typically the same (an example is included in the appendix). However, it is my recommendation that for someone attempting to sell their business it would be a wise investment to have a specific NDA for your business drafted by an attorney.

The main reason I believe this is a justifiable cost is that an attorney will ask you questions about what you would consider to be confidential and what could potentially be harmful to your business if it was learned by others, including competitors. This process will prepare you better for the inevitable concerns you will have about some of this information/data. Also as mentioned before if you have very unique information/data/formulas you might want some extra protection which your attorney could incorporate into your NDA.

Also, as added protection any written documentation should be monitored indicating when it was sent and to whom. My preferred method is to use a virtual data room that logs when people view the data and allows for access control and various levels of security. For the individual business owner selling his business this might not be an option, but you might consider having all data/information transferred first to your attorney and then have them release the information to the approved recipients.

For some small business deals there may be some overkill in these cautions. It will depend on how vulnerable your business could be to harm if the confidential information is misused. I have been involved in deals (such as retail stores) where there was no (or very little) information that was not already available to the public if someone cared. Or the confidential information was not readily available but if someone knew it there was no real harm to the business.

The lengths (and cost) that you go to in this area are based on the level of concerns that exist within your particular business. Always keep in mind that if you limit data/information that legitimate buyers may have access to; they will not buy your business.

8

Negotiations

This is the area that often causes sellers the most concern unless they have a broker or representative to assist. Also, this can be the area where misunderstandings, hurt feelings and personalities can cause a deal to go south.

There are several paths that a deal can take but the most typical would be:

1. Do the analysis to determine market and value. Establish a plan of action to move forward.
2. Prepare the business to be viewed by outsiders.
3. Market the business.
4. Respond to inquiries and answer questions. If an asking price has been established, it is offered here. If not, then any value discussion is delayed.
5. Meet with potential buyers for discussion and possible tour of the business. There are no rules here so this can include detailed discussion. I have always wanted this meeting to be informal and more a meet and greet type meeting with limited details. It will almost always encompass discussions about the future prospects of the business. If the owner cannot lay out a "rosy" future scenario and very positive attitude the deal might not happen.
6. After the meeting there could be verbal discussions (negotiations) regarding additional questions and/or asking price and/or terms, *or*

7. After the meeting there could be a written proposal submitted to the owner. This can be in several forms such as an Indication of Interest or it can be a more formal Letter of Intent. All of these are non-binding.

8. Before any "formal" due diligence or release of more detail data there should be an agreement in principle regarding basic price and terms. And this should be in writing to avoid any misunderstandings. A LOI or an Indication of Intent which will be more detailed than an Indication of Interest should be reviewed by your attorney. While these are almost never binding (except for some aspects related to an exclusive period or non-disclosure aspects) it is important to have a legal review. These documents are subject to negotiations.

9. Once a LOI or Indication of Intent is signed by both parties, due diligence begins. (there is a chapter devoted to due diligence)

10. Often during the time of due diligence, the work will begin on a definite agreement. This is the legally binding document that covers all aspects of the deal. This is negotiated by your attorney.

11. After due diligence depending on the results there can be additional negotiations related to items uncovered during the due diligence and any increased risk. Many deals fall apart at this point because the buyer wants to lower their price from the LOI because of some problem found in due diligence. These are very sensitive and critical negotiations.

12. If everything is fine in due diligence and the deal is still the LOI price (and maybe terms) there is usually negotiations related to the definitive agreement regarding:

Ted Clifton

a. Terms. If this had not been settled at the LOI stage it can be negotiated at this point.
b. Non-competes from sellers.
c. Any employment agreements for sellers or their employees.
d. Escrows/hold backs and how they will be handled.
e. Incentives/Earn-outs related to future performance of the company.
f. Legal issues related to Representations and Warranties.
g. Timing of closing.

Based on the above outline it becomes apparent even in small deals there is room for lots of negotiations. It may be an obvious statement but to have a successful deal happen both sides must want to close. If the dealings become confrontational between the parties or their representatives the likelihood of closing decreases dramatically. Negotiations by their nature often lead to confrontation.

The way to avoid that is to have a clear understanding what you are willing to do and not do. If the buyer says that because they discovered something that changes the value in the business and wants to discuss a price reduction—you must have time to think about what was discovered and if it calls for a price reduction and of course how much. If you are at the bottom number that you are willing to take, then you should be prepared to state that in a non-argumentative way.

As in most things involving business (or maybe just humans) the best approach is to try to reach a compromise. I have seen deals where the deal fell apart because there was a difference that was not a significant amount related to the size of the deal but

51

one side or the other had drawn a line in the sand and would not move. In particular, I remember a $15M transaction that fell apart because of a $500 a month consulting agreement for the seller for 3 years. That was $18,000 in total but both sides had reached the end of their rope and refused to budge—the deal fell apart; everyone lost significant money, many, many times the $18K consulting fee.

Something that I believe helps with negotiations is to use an intermediary (since this book is about not using a broker this could be your lawyer or accountant). This seems to lessen some of those "I shouldn't have said that moments" when you hear something and immediately react. Also, I recommend negotiating in writing. This can slow things down a little, but with email (preferred method) it is not much. Written proposals and counter proposals have the benefit of being in writing (duh!). OK that was a little too obvious; but it is important. Humans have an ability to hear things they want to hear or misunderstand what someone says. It is one thing to negotiate over something everybody understands, it is impossible to negotiate something that was never said that way or meant to convey that fact.

Negotiations are best handled with intermediaries and in writing (email). Also remember there is nothing wrong with taking time to consider all aspects of any proposal and asking for advice from your professional advisors and others.

If you just received communication from the buyer and your first reaction is to immediately get back to that SOB and let him know that is not going to happen; maybe it would be best to wait a day or two and see how you feel. Instant communication is wonderful but can be dangerous.

When negotiations are becoming stressed; it is a good time to bring someone else into the discussion. Always keep your advisors in the loop. Even if your decision is to handle the discussions yourself, keep you advisors informed and up to date on all matters. Somewhere during the deal, it may make a lot of sense to have your advisors step in to handle particularly sensitive discussions.

The goal is to complete the transactions achieving your personal objectives. There are no rules regarding how this has to be done—so adapt as needed to meet the circumstances of the deal.

9
Structuring a Deal

This is an area that can be confusing to many business sellers. The structure of any deal begins with the basics, asset verses equity transaction. Most small deals will be done on an asset basis; larger deals will be done on an equity basis.

What does this mean? An asset deal is the buyer purchasing all of the tangible (physical) and intangible assets of a business. This would be all of the equipment, inventory, vehicles, business name, customer lists, contracts—everything that makes the business run day to day. This can include accounts receivable, patents, and formulas or could be simply the inventory and equipment/leasehold improvements. Each deal will have its own unique list of assets (both tangible and intangible). The important point is that in an asset type deal the buyer is not buying the "legal structure" of the company.

An equity deal is the buyer purchasing the "legal entity" that owns the business and all of the assets of the business. This would be buying the stock/shares in a corporation.

How should a sale be structured?

There is no correct answer to this question. If a deal is structured as an equity transaction the buyer is stepping into the shoes of the seller which can mean assuming liabilities that might or might not be known. This generally has to do with taxes and possible legal actions that might arise after the transaction based on events that occurred prior to the transaction.

The general rule of thumb is that buyers want to purchase assets and sellers want to sell equity. This is based on taxes. If a seller sells equity the taxes associated with the transaction generally are capital gains taxes and much lower than if the deal is done as an asset sale. However, taxes are constantly changing and the impact on the transaction one-year verses another can be different.

This general rule about the structure a buyer wants verses the seller, is over simplified. Many times, a buyer will want to do an equity transaction to allow for a smother transaction. As an example, an asset purchase can/will involve paying sales tax on the assets acquired, it will require re-titling vehicle assets, it will require re-establishing licenses/permits for the company acquiring assets (usually), and it will require much more involvement in the transition phase to make sure that there are not disruptions of the business being acquired.

On the other hand, the equity transaction can be more seamless to employees, customers, regulatory bodies. The biggest problem with the equity type transaction from the buyer's point of view is the risk of contingent liabilities.

Due diligence can give the buyer great assurance he understands and knows everything that has been analyzed and discovered during that process. What can cause a buyer "sleepless nights" is what is not known. No amount of due diligence can uncover an action that may not have occurred yet (IRS audit, new lawsuit being filed about an event that occurred years in the past).

Even the most basic question about how to structure the deal (asset vs equity) is not easy to answer. While the general statements are valid it is important to recognize that each transaction is unique and must be analyzed on its own merits. The analysis and research should involve a legal advisor and a tax advisor.

My advice to most sellers is to try to do an equity deal first. If you cannot find a buyer who will agree to that then examine the asset structure. Remember it probably only means money to the seller. If a buyer wants to do a deal on an asset basis and you are getting enough money to cover the additional taxes involved, if any, then what difference does it make?

The most important element is to be willing to compromise as long as you get your minimum (net) number.

Another aspect of structure is some type of "earn-out". I have had sellers reject this type of structure out of hand. Just would not consider it because they felt it was too speculative. On the other hand, I have put together deals where a large portion of the purchase price was based on earn-outs tied to achieving certain benchmarks. And I have seen those deals work to the benefit of the seller.

As an example, say your target number is $1M and let's ignore taxes and costs. The buyer offers $850K but also offers an earn-out based on reaching certain cash flow objectives (which you consider reasonable) over three years that could generate an additional $100K per year or $300K in total. That would be 15% more than your target number.

But there is risk! Of course, there is risk associated with achieving the target numbers—but if they are reasonable maybe that risk is not so high. There is risk associated with being lied to or defrauded by the buyer after the fact. There are ways to get some protection with the right legal document stating your rights as regards to access to documentation and audit rights. Of course, if your buyer is a crook the legal paperwork may not be worth much.

These contingency payments are a problem for all sides of the deal but can be the key to achieving a deal that offers a win for both sides. The buyer has to have less cash at closing and also gets the comfort of having the seller show confidence in the future financial performance of the business. Many sellers do not hear how it sounds when they say, "I am not taking any future payments—who knows what might happen in the future". The buyer is of course buying the future. The buyer is already very concerned about trying to forecast the future and now the seller is saying no way will he base any of his payments on the future of the business. This does not generate a lot of confidence in the buyer.

On the other hand, the seller hears the buyer say I want to pay you for your business based on some future event—which the buyer controls. So, if the buyer screws up the business, he wants the seller to suffer some economic harm—that does not sound like a good deal to the seller.

My advice is to keep an open mind. Earn-outs can be the glue that will hold a deal together with both sides taking some risk associated with the future to achieve their goals. The worst thing for a seller to do is just reject out-of-hand any idea of earn-outs.

Hold backs represent a portion of the purchase price that is held back at closing until a certain event occurs or a certain amount of time passes. These can take on various forms. Most typically these relate to taxes—these would-be funds held back until a certain time when the threat of audit would pass. They can be related to contingent liabilities that are not known. They can be related to existing lawsuits that have not been settled or the risk of lawsuits not known.

Hold backs represents money owed to the seller after a time period based on no claims against that money arising within that time frame.

Like so much in a business transaction it is not easy to construct a deal that works for everyone. But if you can, then more than likely it is a deal that will happen and provide economic benefit to both sides.

Seller financing is a major consideration on many smaller deals.

Cash is the biggest hurdle for many buyers of smaller businesses. The buyer is limited in the cash available and of course concerned about operating cash after the transaction. Therefor looking for the seller to finance some of the deal is a natural answer to some of the buyers concerns.

Obviously, the seller prefers all cash. I think some sellers become almost unreasonable about this. I have worked some deals where the seller absolutely refused any owner carry and ended liquidating the business for much less money because there was not a buyer who could fund the entire deal. The seller could have gotten as much as he got in liquidation without the hassle and still received a note payable from the buyer for additional consideration. In that case the seller would have been slightly better off whether the buyer paid the note or not—but it became a matter of principle to the seller.

In an ideal situation the seller should receive all (or almost all) of his consideration for the business at closing; but the reality is that most deals will involve some kind of earn-out, hold-back or financing by the seller. Every business will have a different set of facts to deal with and in some cases, financing might not make sense; but with good legal protections, and proper due diligence by the seller it might be what makes the deal happen.

It has been said numerous times but worth repeating; utilize your advisors. Also do not try and do a business deal without the support of legal and tax advisors. Trying to structure a deal regarding asset verse equity, or buy-out options, or financing options or tax considerations would be foolish without having professional advice. These are complicated areas involving potential risks in the future and can only be evaluated after receiving knowledgeable advice from knowledgable advisors.

10
Due Diligence

In the process of selling a business information and data are given to a prospective buyer in order to determine an interest in purchasing the business and to develop an offering value of that business. In some cases, a portion of this information has been reviewed by independent outsiders, such as audited financial statements. In most cases this information/data is not independently verified and is presented without any guarantee that it is correct or complete.

That is what due diligence is about. Most due diligence involves the potential buyer analyzing information/data provided by the seller. There is a sample "due diligence list" included in the appendix for your reference. These lists can be extensive—in that they are trying to cover everything possible. In most cases many of these items will not apply to that particular transaction. Asset transactions will have different due diligence requirements than equity transactions.

Major categories of due diligence by buyer:

1. **Financial statements and supporting documents**. Audited financial statements can eliminate some of the due diligence requirements—in that due diligence auditors can rely upon audit work papers and support schedules from the CPA prepared financial audit. But this is the heart of due diligence making sure that all financial information/data is accurate and complete. This includes looking at details behind the numbers. Many transactions

(especially larger ones) will involve a team of CPA's/accountants who will visit the seller's location and examine a great deal of detail to determine the accuracy and completeness of the financial data. This can be disruptive and very tedious for the seller and their employees/advisors.

2. **Legal**. Another area of concern is legal. This is of course more extensive with an equity transaction. Equity deals will involve extensive legal analysis of the legal entity itself (corporation) and examining all pertinent documents. The level of investigation and document gathering will vary from deal to deal. But this can be an area that takes a significant amount of time to complete. Along with information about the legal entity the buyer will want to know about all legal actions taking against or by the seller and any pending actions that might arise. Once again if this is an equity deal this can be extensive. Attorneys will want to have a complete understanding of any pending legal actions and be able to document the release from all historical legal proceedings. Within legal there will be many requirements for copies of legal documents:

   a. **Real Estate documents/leases**.
   b. **Vehicle titles**.
   c. **Equipment leases**.
   d. **Customer contracts**.
   e. **Employment agreements**.
   f. **Union agreements**.
   g. **Insurance policies**.
   h. **Notes with banks**.
   i. **And more**.

3. **Taxes**. Auditors will want to have a complete handle on all taxes and have all tax returns examined. This will also

include understanding of any tax audits and the risks of future audits. This area will also include documentation related to payment of payroll taxes and all federal, state and local taxes as required.

4. **Licenses and regulatory agencies**. Copies of all business licenses. A complete understanding of all regulation requirements of the company. If the company is subject to regulation this can be a significant area that will be explored. From simple regulation to OSHA, fire regulation, environmental, FDA, FAA and on and on. Each industry will have its own unique regulation environment, and this will be subject to due diligence.

5. **Real Estate**. If real estate (owned or leased) is involved in the transaction this will create a list of due diligence requirements. Environmental is a big issue in this area. Many deals are done where the seller maintains ownership of the real estate and leases it to the buyers to avoid some of the contingency issues related to environmental concerns around real estate.

6. **Assets**. Complete documentation of assets. This can be a list or may be extensive maintenance records. Documentation can include photos and inspections reports. Depending on the type of business this can involve a third-party inspection/valuation report.

7. **Customers**. Besides list of customers and historical detail on revenues, contracts and contacts; often a buyer will want to contact key customers in advance of closing a deal. This can be a very difficult aspect of due diligence. This tends to happen in circumstances where the company has only a few major customers and these customers are critical to the future success of the business. Also, in some

cases customer's contracts will have requirements that the customer must approve any change in ownership related to the continuation of the contract. Obviously, sellers are very concerned about having a potential buyer contact a customer and disrupt the relationship before the deal closes. On the other hand, the buyer will be reluctant to move forward without some assurance that the customers will stay with the company. This takes coordination between seller and buyer to do this in a way that no one is harmed—it can be done. In my dealings I have often found that the customer is only interested in making sure that the same level of service that they have received will continue. This can be aided by the seller remaining with the company for a transition period to assist with any change of ownership issues.

8. **Day to Day operations**. The buyer will want to understand the flow of day-to-day operations. Who does bids? How does the marketing work? This due diligence is somewhat lessened if there is a complete management team that will remain after the change of ownership. If new owners are stepping into key management roles than this is an area that will require extensive due diligence to avoid transition problems.

9. **Employees/Benefits**. In some businesses the most important assets are employees, so it would be obvious that evaluating the employees and examining employee agreements would be a key part of the analysis of the business. This can also involve negotiating new employee agreements with key employees. Once again this is a potential area of conflict between seller and buyer. While the buyer would like to have complete access to all employees the

seller may be reluctant. This can be very tricky, especially if the seller has not informed the employees of the possible transaction. Almost always if the employees are a key part of the business going forward something will have to be worked out where the buyer will have access to at least the key employees. Benefits are also part of due diligence. What is being offered now and what will remain or change after the transactions.

10. **Unions**. If the seller is a union company this is a critical part of due diligence. Examining the contracts between the company and unions and understanding the benefit packages and any potential liabilities associated with deferred liabilities (pensions). There will often be a meeting between a union representative and the buyer.

11. **And Other Stuff**. While this may sound like a catch-all—believe me there will be other stuff. Due diligence is about trying to reach a comfort level that you understand all critical aspects of the transaction and that you have identified all future risks and evaluated their relationship to the deal. Because this involves the future—this will have buyers reaching for all sorts of things trying to find something that will give them additional assurance that they have captured all relevant data. What is acceptable in due diligence is up to the buyer and seller. Nothing is off limits. This of course can create confrontation and cause deals to collapse. My advice to sellers is to expect to be annoyed but provide the info as long as it has some relevance to the deal.

Sellers due diligence is obviously something very different. Usually, a seller only cares about the buyer's ability to pay for the deal and any future obligations. There can of course be other circumstances where a seller would want to analyze the buyer company's stock (if that was to be part of the consideration), or reputation in the industry. Usually, the seller cares about the integrity of the buyer's company beyond just the financial considerations; due to the fact that the seller's employees will become employees of the buyer.

Sellers can ask for financial information about the Buyer Company or individual. The seller can ask for references both for financial matters (banker) and for business practices (customers). Often the seller will do very little beyond getting to know the people involved in the transaction representing the buyer and basing their impressions of the buyer on those contacts.

Buyer due diligence can take days (very small deal with limited assets) to months. The more complicated the deal (equity deal with lots of complications) the longer due diligence takes. For the buyer this can be very expensive. On a medium size deal (sales price of $25M) a buyer can spend $100K to $400K on due diligence. Obviously, the buyer does not want to make a mistake, but this cost is sunk cost if a deal does not happen—so even though there may be some issues or problems arise during due diligence most buyers will want to try and resolve those issues and move forward. There are of course deal killer issues. Generally, those involve major discrepancies between what the buyer has been told and what is really happening. If a buyer finds normal human errors that were obviously unintentional usually that can be resolved—if the buyer finds that there was an attempt to defraud the buyer; they walk away.

A seller should remember that almost anything can be examined during due diligence and if you are trying to hide something more than likely it will come out and cause the deal to collapse.

If you have information that is critical to the business (good or bad) disclose it before it might be uncovered. Even bad news can sometimes be overcome if it is disclosed in a timely manner and there are good explanations for the bad news.

The seller should take very seriously the check list and diligently complete what can be completed as soon as possible. This often involves the seller in managing his support people. This can be employees or outside advisors—but it is up to the seller to manage these people and monitor their progress towards completion. This is a good time for the seller to demonstrate his resolve to completing the process of the sale.

The due diligence process can put a great deal of stress on both parties. The buyer is trying to verify all critical data and find anything that would create issues with the deal; and at the same time keep his costs down and move the deal along in a timely manner. The seller and the seller's employees are stressed with the constant demand for more documents and information. They also feel challenged for any errors (no matter how slight) that might be uncovered.

It is normal for there to be some defensive posturing during this process. It is very important that both sides keep their objective in mind and understand the stress created for everyone.

11
Documents Involved in Closing a Deal

The preparation of the final document (often referred to as a "definitive agreement") will usually begin during due diligence. There are several titles for this type of agreement "Purchase of Business Agreement", "Sale and Purchase Agreement" and "Asset Purchase Agreement". Whatever the name the objective is the same; to layout the various items that have been agreed to by the parties and each party's representations and warranties and obligations.

This agreement can be simple (only a few pages long) or extremely complicated (hundreds of pages long—even thousands with attachments). This is a legal document and, in my opinion, always requires an attorney representing your interests. Even the simple documents should be reviewed by an attorney. This can be a time consuming and expensive process.

The largest issue with this document is making sure you understand what you are agreeing to and how it could impact you in the future. While these documents follow a standard approach and most of the agreements have very common elements there is no standard agreement that has been reviewed and found fair for both parties. Each agreement is unique and requires careful review and understanding.

For most transactions this document becomes the closing document. It is signed and money transferred at the same time. On occasion this document can be signed with a closing date set to a later date. For small deals this is unusual. Once the document is signed the transaction has become binding on both parties; there-fore, to have operations still in the hand of the seller can create some issues related to events that might occur before the actual closing date. For this and other reasons generally this is signed at closing and the business ownership and control transferred at that time.

This document also contains numerous attachments. Once again, the larger more complicated deals can require an amazing number of attachments. But usually, the minimum is a listing of assets, financial statements, list of accounts receivable and pay-able, customer lists, customer contracts, real estate documents, real estate leases, employee agreements, non-competition agreements, insurance documents and more. Most of the attached documents were items that were gathered as part of due diligence. In some cases, these have to be updated for the most current version but generally they should be readily available.

In most deals the agreement is negotiated by the seller's and buyer's attorneys. This is due to the legal nature of the document and the language used. However, both parties will need to under-stand what they are signing. I have mentioned this before, but it is very critical to have an attorney who clearly understands your objectives and an attorney who has the goal of closing the deal. If your attorney's objective is to reduce your risk to zero it could create added risk for the buyer and cause the deal to collapse. The goal is to minimize your risks while still closing the deal and mak-ing sure you understand what you are agreeing to. A good busi-ness attorney is an invaluable asset in this type of transactions—a bad business attorney will prevent the deal from closing and still charge you a fee.

As part of the closing package there is usually a non-competi-tion agreement which is signed by the seller. The buyer is paying for your business (which usually includes goodwill) and will want some market protection from you taking the buyers money and going into competition against the company you sold.

Non-competition agreements usually span 3 to 5 years (although I have seen 10 years) and most generally cover the selling company's market area. I have seen market areas as broad as the entire USA even though the selling company was only in business in a few states. All of these items are of course negotiable. Your attorney can advise you if an agreement overreach. There is a great deal of case law regarding non-competes. The courts have generally ruled that the time and market area covered have to be reasonable for the circumstances. So, buying a business with operations in one state would make a nationwide non-compete seem unreasonable—except if the business is mostly based on a technology or invention that will be taken nationwide by a new owner. Once again this is a legal document, and you will need advice and guidance by your legal advisor.

Employment Agreements can often be part of the closing package. This can be with employees of the seller or with the seller themselves. Many transactions involve the seller staying with the business after the ownership change and managing the business for the new owners. This will almost always require an employment agreement. Employment agreements are unique. There is no universal standard. The agreement lays out the responsibilities of the employee and the employer to each other, the term of employment and the compensation. This can also be an extensive document or a simple one.

Under certain circumstances there can be a separate escrow agreement that is part of the closing package. This is an agreement to a third party who will be holding a portion of the purchase price until a certain event passes or a certain amount of time has passed. The escrow agreement gives specific instructions to the escrow agent as to the circumstances under which the agent would disburse money to the buyer or seller and eventually close the escrow. Normally this escrow agreement will call for the escrow agent to invest the money in some manner and direct the agent on how the earnings are disbursed.

The closing process itself is usually very anticlimactic. The paperwork is signed, money is disbursed, and the deal is done. This process is typically conducted in an attorney's office under the guidance of the attorneys representing each side.

12
Summary

Can you sell your business without a broker? I think the answer to that question is yes. Should you, I am not sure. I know that understanding all aspects of a business transaction will assist you in the process whether you use a broker or not.

This book has detailed some of the items you will encounter while selling your business. There are of course many things that can occur while you are putting your business on the market—some of which we have not discussed. Most of the frustration in selling a business revolves around having to deal with people who are not competent or able financially to actually buy a business. This can not only be very annoying but time consuming.

One of the risks is that you become so involved in selling your business you do not manage the business the way you should. If you are an absentee owner this is not a problem; but if you are the main person responsible for the business operation day to day being distracted with meetings with buyers or attorneys can end up costing you. Even to the point of damaging the business enough that it cannot be sold.

I think one of the most important aspects of doing this yourself is to set reasonable goals and fully understand the additional cost that will be involved. The goal must give you the time to spend on selling the business but also keep you engaged in running the business. The additional cost is for everything that might be required: attorneys, additional accounting work, additional employees to help with the workload you may not be able to handle, marketing materials, additional legal work, business valuation, market analysis and more.

We have covered most of the major items you will need to understand and accomplish:

- **Timing.** Yes, it is everything. Selling your business involves making the decision to sell based on understanding the market and knowing how buyers look at businesses. Unless you want to sell your business at a steep discount you need to sell when everything is looking good. If you look at your business and say I don't want to sell now because everything is looking to good—*that is when you should sell!*
- **Personal Objective.** Do not put your business on the market to "just test the waters". That will not work. You need to establish your personal reasons for selling and stick with them. Once the timing is right it should be your total objective to sell the business. You should have established your reasons; retirement, health, other business interest, cashing out to establish more leisure time, fund your kid's education or just tired of the day-to-day grind and want to live on the beach. Set your goal of selling within a certain time frame (2 years) and start the process—do not waiver.
- **Do the research.** Identify the buyers. If it is a small business and there are no national/major buyers identify attributes that the typical buyers of your type of business will have. Prepare your marketing plan. Put together a plan of action that details how you will go about identifying and contacting potential buyers. Planning will help you think about what the buyer will be like and how to find them.
- **Know the value of your business.** Understand what creates value in a business. Either do a business valuation yourself or

hire someone to do it. At the very beginning you need to know what your business might be worth and if this is the amount you are willing to sell for. Do not mislead yourself. If you want $X for your business but it is only worth half of that—you will not find someone to give you $X. It will not happen. Understanding what creates value also helps you design your marketing strategy to emphasize those qualities about your company that will attract a buyer.

- **Be prepared to share information.** You cannot sell your business in a vacuum. Buyers want information/data; often more than seems reasonable. Understand this and be ready for it—have the information ready to go and in a form that is easy for the buyer to understand. Put together your confidentiality agreement. Draft your one-page blind summary. Assemble your selling memorandum.
- **Put your team together.** To complete a business sale will almost always involve a lawyer and an accountant. If you already have these people aboard, meet with them and discuss your objectives and listen to their advice. If you do not have these professionals do the research and find the people who can provide these services and will assist you in the process.

This book obviously cannot cover everything that might happen in the process of selling a business. I have been engaged in this industry for over 30 years and every year something will happen that surprises me. What I wanted to do was give you the background to understand the pieces of the puzzle. You should now know all of the major elements involved in selling a business.

The size of the deal is very significant. If you are a middle market company your transaction will involve almost every complication, there is in a deal and require you to be fully engaged in the process with a strong team of advisors. Smaller businesses can be (most generally are) much less complicated and time consuming. The small deal issue is finding a buyer. Once a qualified buyer is found the process is much less complicated as opposed to the larger deals.

The structure of the deal will add to the simplicity or complication of the process. Equity deals add time to due diligence and can be much more complicated legally than asset deals. Having multiple sellers can complicate and add to due diligence. Debt structure or excess working capital can create additional concerns to be addressed.

We have dealt with some of these complications but not all. Each deal, each seller and each buyer will bring their own uniqueness's and complications to the transaction. If you have done your homework, research and proper meditation then you are ready to sell your business without a broker. Lots of luck!

2-for-1 Bonus:

How to Value a Small Business

Introduction

This series addresses the often-asked question of how to determine the value of a privately held small business. The problem is that there is usually a lack of good data to use as a comparison. Unlike the real estate market where there are many transactions and most often those transactions are public in some nature, a small business sell is less common and usually the information from that transaction is not available to outside parties. So how do you determine the value of a small closely held business? This series will address some of the factors that determine value and some of the techniques used by people who do valuations. This series will not tell you the value of your business. After we have covered all aspects of determining value you may feel that you are better qualified to understand what drives value and maybe even knowledgeable enough to estimate the value of your business. That would be well and good. But this course is not about becoming a business valuator nor is it about teaching the business owner to determine the value of his business. It is about you learning how it is done.

What we will cover:

- **Course One: The basics**. What determines value? How public companies can sometimes seem to be valued without regard to the company's financial condition. What you will need to

---

know about a small privately held company to determine value.

- **Course Two: Risk drives everything**. Understanding and trying to measure risk determines value. How to measure risk. What are some of the characteristics of high risk and low risk? Why are some industries considered low risk and others high risk?

- **Course Three: Reward is what you get for taking risks**. What type of reward enters into measuring value? How is reward different then owner's compensation? How to adjust the reward analysis for owners comp. What are considered "normal" rewards for relative risks?

- **Course Four: Financial statement recasting**. What does it mean? Why are statements restated? How can one owner be different in his analysis as opposed to another? What are usually considered add backs?

- **Course Five: Methods of income and benefit used in analysis**. What is owner's discretionary income? How is this used to determine value in small businesses? What are earnings before interest and taxes (EBIT) and earnings before interest, taxes, depreciation and amortization? Other types of income/earnings used in analysis.

- **Course Six: Valuing Intangibles**. What are intangibles? Why is it important to place a value on intangibles? What aspects of a business increase/decrease the value of intangibles?

- **Course Seven: Methods used to arrive at value**. Capitalization of earnings. Discounting future benefits.

- **Course Eight: Capitalization rates and discount rate**. How they are calculated and what they mean to the value of a business.

- **Course Nine: Sample valuations**. Will show the same company with the same set of facts value in different ways with

remarkably different results.
- **Course Ten: Conclusions.**

Our objective is to provide you with sufficient understanding to know what contributes to value in your business and what doesn't. This course is not all-inclusive and only attempts at a core understanding of the subject matter. Enjoy!

Course One
The Basics

The value of any business is actually a very simple concept. But while simple in theory it is often difficult to actually determine. Value is based on the ability of a business to generate a stream of funds into the future. Or in other words how profitable will this business be in the years ahead.

If you could predict with complete accuracy the future profits (or cash flow) of a business, you could easily determine its value. By knowing the future income stream, the value would be based on the investors (buyers) desired return as compared to other investment alternatives. So, if a business could generate $100,000 per year return to its owner without the owner's active involvement and with some reasonable assurance that this would occur every year; the buyer might say the business was worth $1,250,000 which would be an 8% return on his investment. Simple.

Now the problem; nobody knows the future. And with businesses you better believe you do not know the future. You could have a company with a consistent track record of increased profits for the last twenty years, and in the twenty-first year lose money! The reasons could be management, your product is suddenly obsolete, the global economy, the national economy, the local economy, the weather, the stars; you name it, and it can affect business.

So, if determining the value of a business is based on predicting the future, you probably should go see a physic rather than a business consultant, right? Well maybe! The answer you get could be as useful. However, there are ways of determining a "good guess" at the future performance of a business, the past. Keeping in mind the example above of the company with a consistent twenty-year profitable track record and then losing in the twenty-first; nevertheless, in most cases the past is a very good indicator of the future. A company that has been in business twenty years is going to be a lot easier to forecast into the future than one that has been in business only a few years.

The quality and quantity of historical information enters into an analysis that determines the "risk" associated with the future of a business. The elements that determine risk are as numerous as the elements that effect a business performance; the global to local economies, competition, management stability, management skills, capital requirements, cost of capital, product/service stability, customer demographics, supplier's stability, location of the business and on and on.

Therefore, in the simplest of terms a business is worth its ability to generate future profits (or cash flow) modified by a risk factor, which incorporates all elements of risk associated with predicting and producing those future profits. Easy to say, hard to calculate.

Shannon P. Pratt, a widely recognized valuation authority, describes this theory and its complications more elegantly:

> *A generally accepted theoretical structure underlies the process of valuing a business interest. In theory, the value of an interest in a business depends on the future benefits that will accrue to it, with the value of the future benefits discounted back to a present value at some appropriate discount (capitalization) rate. Thus, the theoretically correct approach is to project the future benefits (usually earnings, cash flow, or dividends) and discount the projected stream back to a present value.*
>
> *However, while there is general acceptance of a theoretical framework for business valuation, translating*

it into practice in an uncertain world poses one of the
most complex challenges of economic and financial theory
and practice.[2]

Some of this may sound like gobbledygook, but if you are a seller or a buyer of a business it is important to understand the concepts of value. The value of your business may be determined by an industry specific rule-of-thumb or many other methods that attempt to simplify the basics described above into something that is easier to calculate and understand. But it will be based on the basic principle of future benefits modified by a risk factor. Understanding this puts you in a better position to make a deal that works for you.

As we have recently seen in some of the more bizarre examples with .com public companies, value is based on a perception of the future. While the more dramatic examples of this tend to occur in publicly traded companies where individual investors may not be risking a large portion of their personal wealth, this is still a valid concept with privately held businesses. A business is worth what a "buyer/investor" perceives as future reward associated with the business. A business that has a unique concept or product will have a much higher "perceived" value to investor/buyers than a ho-hum business model.

The challenge to the valuator is to be able to understand and translate "sizzle" into value without overstating the future potential of an unproven business. The easiest business to value is one with a proven, stable track record; the hardest is one with great (but unproven) potential.

---

2   Shannon P. Pratt, *Valuing a Business, The Analysis and Appraisal of Closely Held Companies*, Second Edition (Dow Jones-Irwin, 1981 and 1989), p. 35.

Course Two
Risk Drives Everything

Risk is the nemesis that must be recognized in business. When you go into a new business you are risking your investment of time and money. How much risk? Everyone has probably had someone offer them an investment in some scheme that was "just too risky" to consider. How that determination was made, whether intuitive or analytical, is at the heart of measuring the value of a business.

As we said in the last session if we were assured a certain return in a business venture it would not be difficult to calculate the value of that business. You would only have to determine what an acceptable rate of return would be and do the math. So, if a business would generate $100,000 per year before taxes with *no risk* what would the value of that business be? Depending upon competing investment opportunities we might say that the value of that investment might be $1,500,000. That would be a before tax return of about 7%. If there was *no risk* a before tax return of 7%, during certain times, might attract significant investment.

On the other hand, there are no small privately held businesses that do not have risk. Matter of fact most of these businesses have very high risk. To demonstrate the impact of the risk factor let's take the same numbers as above and say the risk factor is 35%. We will discuss how we can estimate risk in a little bit. So, at a risk factor of 35% the $100,000 in income would be worth $285,000. We went from a value of $1,500,000 to a value of $285,000 on the same income based on risk.

If you are a business owner this is a very powerful concept to understand. How risk is measured and hence how it effects the value of your business. Certain industries have perceptions of risk and as a result there is only so much a business owner can do to affect the value of his business in those industries. However even the highest risk industries will vary tremendously within the industry group. For example, restaurants. This is obviously a very high-risk business. Almost everyone knows someone, or a relative of someone, who has failed in the food service industry. The reasons are numerous and go beyond our scope here. But suffice it to say this is an industry that goes through boom-and-bust cycles during the best of times. Even when other industries are doing exceptionally well there will be restaurants going out of business. It is just the nature of the beast that the failure rate in restaurants is high.

But within this high-risk business there are going to be restaurants that will rate at much higher risk than others. Now the obvious element is size. A large operation with significant capital invested is less risky than a small mom and pop, right? Well not necessarily. Size is a factor in success but usually measured by the number of units. If you have the resources to expand your restaurant from a single location than you improve your odds of overall success. This seems to be a factor due to circumstances that can hinder one location and cause it to decline in business even when the owners are doing everything right. Such as road construction, or some other act of god or government, that causes the business to fail. So, you should never have one restaurant, you should always open 2 or 3 or 5? The answer is yes, if you want to lower risk.

If you do not have the capital to open 5 restaurants rather than one, how else could you lower risk? Good documentation is a good way to lower risk. The better your record keeping the more accurate your decisions about your business. Especially if you were trying to sell your business; good records have a lot to do with being able to measure the risk of the business in the future. Besides record keeping would be good documentation on the day-to-day operation of the business. While no small business owner wants to spend time developing these operational type materials it will have a lot to do with the risk of the business failing. I think this is common sense. The better documentation you have the better your business is managed. The better it is managed the more profitable it will be. Therefore, someone might measure the risk of the business maintaining a profitable operation into the future by looking at your operational documentation.

Another factor that drives risk in restaurants and most businesses is employees. While employees do not show up on a balance sheet as a business asset, they usually are the businesses biggest assets. Well trained and well-paid employees will provide stability to a business that will decrease the risk associated with the business.

Understanding the concept of risk in establishing value for a business is to understand what is inherently risky about business. You will not find a business that does not have risk. Some businesses have less risk and as a result will be "worth" more in relationship to their income. A good example would be income producing real estate. Because of the stability (and scarcity) of real estate and that usually the income is contractually based; income producing real estate will have some of the lowest risk factors in business.

For example, if we assumed two businesses producing $100,000 per year benefit to their owners (lots of details here we are ignoring to make a point); one an apartment building and one a trendy new restaurant serving squid tacos. The apartment building might have a cap rate of 10% (we will discuss cap rates in a future session) that would give it a value of $1,000,000. The restaurant might have a cap rate of 40% that would give it a value of $250,000. Two business both generating $100,000 to their owners one worth 25% of the other one. That is due to risk.

Actually, we should say that is due to the *perception* of risk. No one can know the future for sure (first lesson); so, values are driven by perceptions of the future. It is this fact that can cause such significant swings in value from one industry to another. An industry that is "perceived" to be strong in the future will have a higher current value based on actual performance than one that is perceived to be weak. As a result, you can have some "old economy" type industries valued at rather low factors of their earnings and companies engaged in "new economy" speculation value at perceptions that don't make much sense.

When someone is hired to value a privately held small business one of the key factors, they need to determine will be a risk factor. This risk factor analysis becomes the capitalization rate and discount rate to determine value. One of the methods used is called a build-up method. Which takes key elements of a business and assigns a rating or percentage based on the risk for that particular business. This model will begin with a risk-free rate (say 6%) and add additional percentage points based on the analysis by the valuator. An example might be:

        6.0 Risk Free
        2.0 Management
        4.0 Industry
        3.0 Key Employees
        1.0 Marketing
        1.0 Facilities
        1.5 Record Keeping
       18.5 Total

For this business the risk factor or capitalization rate might be 18.5%. Without knowing anything about the business we can see that the valuator thought the industry had slightly higher risk, management was pretty good, maybe missing a key employee, but the business had good marketing, facilities and bookkeeping. Keep in mind that another evaluator might come up with an entirely different set of numbers. While there have been some tremendous improvements in the quality of business valuations there is still a great deal of judgment that enters into the decision.

While professional valuators would like to be able to eliminate "judgment" and replace it with scientific formulae, the real-world deals with this judgment every day. Much of the risk analysis that is done regarding a small business is intuitive. Someone trying to buy a small business will make these intuitive judgments in determining what they offer for the business. A good example is reflected in my experiences as a business broker. If a business had a well-kept building, there was a perception that management was doing a good job. I was specifically told on a multiple million-dollar deal that one of the main reasons the buyer went forward with the deal was the housekeeping of the plant. What that buyer was doing was assigning a lower risk factor to that business using intuition because of the way they maintained their physical plant.

Course Three
Reward is What You Get for Taking Risks

As we said in lesson two "risk" is the nemesis that must be recognized in business. Every business has risk. So why invest money and time into a business that has risk. The answer is reward. As businesspeople we risk our money and our time to achieve a greater success. That reward is usually more money. Although there are some situations where the reward is a combination of money and intangibles. For our purposes we will stick with the tangible reward of money or wealth. Invest $100,000 in something you expect to receive a return for your investment. As we discussed in the last session your expectation of return will have to do with the risk of your investment.

So, if you invest your $100,000 in a government insured certificate of deposit at a local bank you would expect your return or reward to be relatively small. That type of investment is going to be relatively liquid (you can get you money on fairly short notice) and low risk, thus a low return. However, if you invested your money with your next-door neighbor who has convinced you that he has discovered a new way of catching mice you would expect a much higher return on your investment. Higher risk equals higher return.

With investments this concept is fairly straightforward. As a passive investor you provide your capital and expect a certain return. Also, as a passive investor you can compare competing investments based on perceptions of risks and potential returns. If two banks were offering $100,000 thirty-day CD, one at 4% and one at 5%, it would not be a difficult decision to select which one to invest your $100,000. However, if you were trying to decide between the bank CD and a much riskier stock investment there would be many other factors to consider. Those factors would relate to risk and reward associated with the competing investments.

A small business investment is a much more complicated situation. The complications are affected by two main points (i) a lack of liquidity and (ii) active participation by the investor.

When you make an investment, you anticipate that you will receive a return (reward) for your investment plus you will receive your investment back at some point in the future. As in our example if you invest $100,000 in a bank CD you expect to receive interest and your $100,000 back. Or if you invested in a public company you might expect to receive dividends but most assuredly you would expect to be able to sell your investment for more than you paid.

When you invest in a small business you will also expect to receive a return on a regular basis and to be able to sell your investment at some time. This is a key issue in placing a value on a small business. Can it be sold? The market for small closely held businesses does exist but it is not organized nor is it a disciplined market. As a result, predicting the sale of any individual small business can be very problematic.

At our consulting firm we spend a great deal of time advising clients about this area. We you go into a business have some idea how you will get out. In order to maximize your investment, you must be able to exit from your business. If you plan this exit strategy going in you are in a much better position to achieve a successful exit, then if you wait until you need to sell your business.

This lack of marketability will come into play in many valuations of small closely held businesses. Often a business valuator will discount (or decrease) the value of a business due to this lack of marketability. Obviously being able to sell your business is a key element in its value.

Another key element in most business valuations is the owner's involvement and his or her compensation. The owner (investor) not only invests money into the business but also time. The money investment can usually be tracked and documented. But often the time commitment is more difficult to measure. If an owner consistently works 70-hour weeks for half of a "normal" manager wages what is the investment of that owner. Plus, what is the reward from that same business if the owner at the end of the year shows a $100,000 profit?

As we will see in the next session recasting or restating financial information is an important part of determining the value of a small business. That is usually due to the type of situation we described above. And also, the owner will often take out additional compensation in ways other than as a salary. The owner in the above example expenses several automobiles through the company and "writes-off" a business trip to Hawaii every year. This often becomes the biggest challenge of the business valuator; what is the actual reward that this business is generating to the owner?

The actual reward might be calculated as follows:

$100,000 Business Income
-50,000 Less adjustment to owner's compensation to equal normal salary
-20,000 Cost to replace additional time by owner
+15,000 Plus owner's "perks"
$45,000 Business Return

After restatement (recasting) the business is generating a return (pre-tax) of $45,000 for the capital invested. We went from a $100,000 return to a $45,000 return by understanding what a reward is and what is an investment.

The owner of a small closely held business has many "opportunities" to affect the financial performance of his or her business. To understand value, it is imperative that the financial data and operational data be examined to recognize adjustments that need to be made. Sometimes this is called "normalizing" earnings. To adjust the actual financial data to reflect the operation without the "unusual" items that might affect in particular period.

This is an area of much confusion and disagreement. Often a seller of a business will identify one-time operational issues that have had a negative impact on the business and want them adjusted back into the profit mix. A buyer will say that those so-called one-time expenditures are really just a normal cost of business and should be deducted to determine profits. This can create a wide difference of opinion as to what "normalized earnings" actually should be.

Adding to this confusion is the fact that many different types of earnings are often used as the basis for determining value. We will cover this aspect further in session five. Some valuation models will use pre-tax income, or after-tax income, or earnings before interest and taxes (EBIT) or earnings before interest, taxes, depreciation and amortization (EBITDA). These are all simply measures of reward to the owner of the business.

While reward may come in many ways in owning a small closely held business, our concern regarding valuations is to measure the intangible reward that results from the investment in that business.

Combining this reward determination with our assessment of

risk will start to lay the foundation to determine value.

Worth mentioning at this point is a brief discussion of rules-of-thumb. We will discuss this subject in greater detail in a later session, but at this point I would like to look at this most simple of valuation models. A rule-of-thumb is a simple method that is industry specific that takes a relationship between value and some common aspect of the business. This is usually a percentage of annual revenues (or multiple of monthly or annual revenues), a multiple of earnings (or some form of earnings) or possibly a multiple of some measure of unit unique to that industry (a value times the number of gallons sold).

These rules-of-thumb are based on collective data from that industry. As such they can be very informative in that they are based on market information. The biggest weakness (and therefore concern) is that they are based on averages and do not address specific circumstances of individual businesses.

Underlining all rule-of-thumbs are basic assumptions about risk and reward. The formula may end up being simple such as one times annual revenues but built into that simplistic is the basic concept of return on investment and alternative investment options.

Course Four
Financial Statement Recasting

As we saw in the last session recasting or restating financial information is an important part of determining the value of a small business. That is usually due to the type of situation we described in the previous session, where the owner is being paid half of a normal mangers wages and consistently working 70-hour workweeks. And usually, the small business owner will be taking out additional compensation in ways other than as a salary. The owner in our previous example was deducting expenses for several automobiles through the company and was "writing-off" a business trip to Hawaii every year. This often becomes the biggest challenge of the business valuator; what is the actual reward that this business is generating to the owner?

In our previous example the reward or return was recalculated to be:

$100,000 Business Income
 -50,000 Less adjustment to owner's compensation to equal
         normal salary
 -20,000 Cost to replace additional time by owner
 +15,000 Plus owner's "perks"
 $45,000 Business Return

After restatement (recasting) the business is generating a return (pre-tax) of $45,000 for the capital invested. We went from a $100,000 return to a $45,000 return by understanding what a reward is and what is an investment.

The owner of a small closely held business has many "opportunities" to affect the financial performance of his or her business. To understand value, it is imperative that the financial data and operational data be examined to recognize adjustments that need to be made. Sometimes this is called "normalizing" earnings. To adjust the actual financial data to reflect the operation without the "unusual" items that might affect in particular period.

This is an area of much confusion and disagreement. Often a seller of a business will identify one-time operational issues that have had a negative impact on the business and want them adjusted back into the profit mix. A buyer will say that those so-called one-time expenditures are really just a normal cost of business and should be deducted to determine profits. This can create a wide difference of opinion as to what "normalized earnings" actually should be.

This process of recasting financial statements is a major element in determining value of most closely held small businesses. Large companies and especially public companies are subject to exacting standards on how they keep their books. Larger companies must adhere to a set of standards referred to as Generally Accepted Accounting Principles or GAAP. These standards are devised by the accounting gurus and monitored by auditors. All public companies and most larger organizations have their financial information examined by independent auditors who state whether those statements adhere to GAAP and present fairly the financial condition of the company.

Small business is a different story. As a consulting firm it is the area of consistent weakness we see in small businesses. A lack of quality financial information to make decisions. This is usually due to budget considerations and quite often just a lack of understanding by the business owner of the dire consequences of not dedicating adequate resources to this vital function. A small business owner will often maintain records primarily to file income tax returns. So, one of the big challenges in determining value is to have a good set of financial statements that reflect the financial condition of the business.

Since few small businesses share their financial information with anyone other than maybe a banker and the IRS, they will often maintain their records on a tax basis. This usually means that they are keeping their books on a cash basis.

Cash basis financial statements present a very incomplete picture of the financial conditions of smallest businesses. Now if you happen to be a service business with no inventory who only does business for customers on a cash basis and pays all of your bills when you receive the service or product then maybe the cash basis statements accurately reflect your business. However, for most businesses these statements are incomplete and occasionally misleading.

Another factor in small businesses is that the business owner is usually motivated to minimize taxes. As a result, the owner may make decisions based on the tax timing or tax consequences as opposed to decisions to maximize profits. This can result in the understatement of earnings by the business or at the very least a cloudy picture as to the earnings potential of the business.

For these reasons most small businesses need to have their financial data restated or recasted to establish a more accurate picture of the financial performance of the business. This recasting requires analysis and interpretation. This can be and often is a point of contention between parties with different interests.

If you are a seller of a business trying to establish value, you will want as many dollars as possible added-back to your financial statement to improve your company's profitability and thus its value. On the other hand, if you are a buyer you will questions all add-backs and look for items that should be deducted from earnings and thus lowering value. This tug-of-war is usually part of the negotiation process in buying and selling a business.

Someone independently placing value on a business must use their best judgment to determine what should be adjustments to the financial statements of the company being valued. There can be significant disagreement between valuators regarding the legitimacy of these types of adjustments with dramatically different results.

There is not a standard list of items that should or should not be added-back or considered adjustments to financial statements. Some of these we have already discussed related to owner's compensation and perks. Some items that might need to be examined:

- **Owner's salary.** This can be where the owner is withdrawing excess compensation and understating profits or where the owner is contributing his services below "normal" wages and overstating profits.
- **Owner's perks and discretionary expenditures.** Some items could be add-backs because they are not considered part of the business operations (a Hawaii vacations) while others could be adjustments because they were excessive and discretionary (such as luxury vehicles as company cars).
- **Unusual and/or one-time expenditures.** If you are trying to determine "normal" earnings than anything that occurred in the based year you are examining that is not "normal" could be an adjustment. This can also be an unusual or one-time occurrence that is beneficial to the company. Such as a gain on the sale of an asset or receipt of insurance proceeds.
- **Interest expense.** In most cases small business valuations are made on the basis of a debt free analysis. Therefore, interest

expense (if deducted from operations) is added back.

Also, in many valuation models depreciation and amortization are added back. These models look at these "expenditures" as non-cash outlays during that period.

Hopefully you are starting to see that the valuation of a small business involves many variables. We must assess risk and then be able to measure reward or return. These simple concepts can become very complicated in the real world with real businesses.

Course Five
Methods of Income/Benefit Used in Analysis

In the previous sessions we have discussed risk and reward relationships as the basis of value. We have also mentioned some different earnings/benefits that are used in the calculation of small business values. These different bases: such as net income, pre-tax earnings, earnings before interest and taxes (EBIT) and earnings before interest, taxes, depreciation and amortization (EBITDA) are common measures used by small and large businesses alike.

One measure, owner's discretionary income, is unique to small businesses. The method using this approach is called the Multiple of Discretionary Earnings Method. The reason this measure and the market driven data supporting this as a basis of valuation came about is quite simple. Data from most small businesses is heavily skewed by owner's compensation. It is either too high or too low. In most cases it involves benefits that would not be afforded the average manager. As a result, most measures did not make sense unless you made adjustments for owner's comp and benefits. Therefore, why not just use the number before any of the owner's consideration is deducted which is called owner's discretionary income. With this approach there became available data from market transactions based upon this income number.

Plus, much of the decision about buying small businesses is based more on what you can take out as opposed to a more sophisticated return on investment analysis. Someone might think in terms of valuing a business based on the income they think they can make. So, someone might think that they would pay $300,000 for a business if they can make a $60,000 income for themselves. On the surface that might look like a 20% return, but if the owner will work in the business and he values his worth (as an employee/manager) at $60,000; he is not making anything for his $300,000 investment. That is not a good deal—but buyers, based on such logic, value many businesses.

Some of this is in the area of intangibles. The owner might be willing (assuming he has it!) to pay $300,000 for a business because he wants the personal satisfaction of owning his own business. Or maybe the owner feels the value of the business will grow substantially in the future justifying his investment. These are all considerations when placing a value on a business.

Another area that causes come concern with this approach is a lack of standard definitions of the terms used to define the method. The International Business Brokers Association (IBBA) defines some of the related terms as:

Owner: A generic term used in business brokerage to represent the proprietor, general partner, or controlling shareholder (singular or plural as appropriate).

Owner's Salary. The salary or wages paid to the owner, including related payroll tax burden.

Owner's Total Compensation. Total of owner's salary and perquisites.

Perquisites. Expenses incurred at the discretion of the owner, which are unnecessary to the continued operation of the business.

This method evolved from a general "rule-of-thumb" for small businesses that the value could be calculated as "one times owner's cash flow, plus the market value of the tangible assets." Much of the logic for that formula found its basis in asset-based businesses, such as retailers with inventory intensive businesses. Service business would tend to be undervalued.

Today there are market-based databases that supply market comparisons on the basis of a multiple of owner's discretionary income (or cashflow). This information if used properly can be very useful. However, users need to be very careful that they understand the definitions used in the data gathering and also how tangible assets are handled. In some cases, some assets (inventory, accounts receivable) are added back to the multiple of discretionary income and sometimes they are not.

The simplicity of this approach makes it attractive, but that same simplicity can make the information derived from this approach wrong.

Large publicly held businesses usually do not have that kind of problem. These businesses are valued in the marketplace by an active market of many investors. This market will place premiums on certain characteristics and punish others. The public marketplace uses many of the earnings numbers we have discussed, such as EBIT and EBITDA, to establish values for public companies. For many types of industries, a multiple of EBIT or EBITDA has become a "rule of thumb" to establish value.

The most common benchmark that we see with public companies is an Earnings Per Share multiple. These earnings multiple is often quoted as part of the financial data presented for a public company. It is tempting for small business owners to try and make some comparisons about their business and a large public company on the basis of these types of measures. I have had small business owners say to me "if ABC Big Company, Inc. is worth 30 times their earnings why isn't my company even worth 10 times"?

The most important thing to remember about these various measures is that they are benchmarks. Their only meaning is as a comparison. And each of these measures whether for large public companies or small "mom and pops" needs to be defined very specifically on who they are being calculated. A small business might sell for 3 times EBITDA plus tangible assets or it might sell for 6 times EBITDA including tangible assets; but when the "news" gets into the marketplace one might have sold for 3 times cash flow and the other 6. But until you have all of the facts you would not know which was the best deal.

Course Six
Valuing Intangibles

As a broker I have had many conversations where a buyer will tell me he is not paying for blue sky. It is obvious the buyer does not understand what creates value in a business. Of course, no buyer would do this, but if you followed the logic of the no blue-sky statement a buyer would be willing to pay the same value for a business losing $100,000 per year as one making a $100,000 per year.

Blue Sky means something of no value and has its basis in securities law. Many people use the term "Blue Sky" as if it was interchangeable with "Goodwill"—which it is not. Goodwill is more of an accounting term meaning something *of value* that is not tangible, usually associated with the intangible value of a business. The Goodwill of a business is the value associated with the businesses ability to generate a return on its tangible assets over and above a benchmark rate. A business that could generate a 30% return on its equity would have more Goodwill value than a business that could only generate a 15% return.

This would reflect the "value" of good customer relations, quality of employees, business reputation, brand identity, market dominance, product uniqueness, patents and many more. Taken in total this would be the intangible value of a business. Some of these areas can be valued independently of the business operation, such as patents, but generally these intangibles only have value as they relate to the on-going business.

In the small business world, which is our focus, the intangible value can often be associated with the owner of the business. This can create a difficult problem in establishing a value of the business. How much of the intangible value (or Goodwill) of the business will be lost if the owner leaves? In many cases when buyers of small businesses say they will not pay for Goodwill, it is that concern that they are expressing. They do not want to pay a premium for a business based on the owner and then have the owner leave. Also, from a valuation point-of-view it is impossible to separate an active owner's contributions to improve performance and what would be Goodwill that would stay with the business under different ownership.

If you are a small business owner and you are trying to create Goodwill value, there are several areas you should look at:

- Create value in the business not in yourself. This means to try and establish a business identity that is separate from you. You may be the key employee/worker/manager but think of the business as a separate entity.
- If your business is large enough make it a priority to develop key employees. Other than the obvious benefit of better day-to-day operations, key employees establish value within the business. Employees are often the most important factor in being able to exit (sell) your business at the best value.
- Document everything. The more and better documentation you have the more your business has its own identity. If you keep all of the rules, procedures, methods etc. in your head, your business is totally dependent upon you and it will be hard to build Goodwill value associated with the business itself.
- Do not become a slave to your business. If you have not taken a vacation in several years you are probably decreasing the "value" of your business—not to mention the value of your life.
- If at all possible, join a program where other businesspeople can make suggestions about your business. A good way to cre-

ate value in your business is to be open to outside input. This does not have to be expensive. We participate in a chamber of commerce program to be very beneficial in this regard and it only costs $100 per year.

One of the most common business valuation techniques is based upon the logic of intangible value being measurable. That is the Excess Earning Method. This method originated in 1920 with the publication of Appeals and Review Memorandum 34 by the U.S. Department of the Treasury. And has been updated with IRS Revenue Rulings.

The basic assumption underlying the Excess Earnings Method is that business profit in excess of a "normal" rate of return on tangible assets is produced by intangible assets. These "excess earnings" can be capitalized into intangible value or goodwill. The steps for applying the method would be:

1. Determine the value of the tangible operating assets and liabilities.
2. Determine the "representative" operating profit.
3. Determine the required rates of return for the tangible operating assets. These rates are used to calculate a return on tangible assets component, which is subtracted from the representative operating profit to derive "excess earnings."
4. Determine the required rate of return for the intangible assets. This rate is used to calculate intangible asset value, or "goodwill." The total business value can then be found by combining the value of the goodwill with the net tangible asset value determined in Step 1.

The capitalization rates used as examples in the rulings were 15 to 20 percent. It has been suggested that the cap rates should range from 20 to 100 percent. We will go into cap rates in greater depth in course eight.

There is no question that there are real world limitations on what someone is willing to pay for Goodwill. Some of this limitation is based on the fact that it is hard to measure the Goodwill contribution into the future. This is of course especially true in small business. If we could agree that the Goodwill portion of income being derived from a business is $50,000 per year, how many years of that Goodwill would I be willing to pay for? After a certain point I would feel like it was my efforts that would be creating Goodwill. If I were unwilling to pay more than 5 times for the Goodwill than the minimum cap number would be 20 percent.

Understanding the basis for Goodwill and how to improve your businesses Goodwill value can be a significant contributor to increasing the value of your business. Also understanding Goodwill can be a major benefit if you are looking to buy a business.

Course Seven
Valuation Methods

As we have gone through this series, we have mentioned several different methods used to value businesses: Excess Earnings Method, Rule of Thumbs, Market Methods, Multiple of Discretionary Earnings Method and others. In this session we are going to discuss several methods used by valuators to determine value. As we said at the beginning the purpose of this series is not to make you an appraiser but to give you some basic understanding of the process so you can use that knowledge to your advantage.

The methods we will briefly discuss are:

- Asset-based Methods
- Capitalization of Earnings Method.
- Multiple of Discretionary Earnings Method.
- Rules of Thumb
- Excess Earnings Method.
- Discounted Future Earnings Method.

One of the first premises we set forward was that a business was valued based on its ability to generate a benefit to its owner *in the future*. The value of a business today is not what it has done in the past but what it will do in the future. However, we use past performance as an indicator of how the business will perform in the future. I mention this because there is really only one of the above methods that actually estimate a business financial performance into the future, that is the Discounted Future Earnings Method. The other methods use other ways (capitalization rates) to account for the risk associated with the future.

This is the major weakness in all business valuations methods. Even if you do not use a projection of financial performance method such as the Discounted Future Earnings Method, you are still estimating the future in one fashion or another. And any estimate of the future requires the person doing the estimate to make certain assumptions. Many business valuators would like to pretend that most of the valuation process could be made to adhere to scientific application. In my opinion the process of placing a value on a closely held small business still involves a tremendous amount of "art" along with the scientific aspects.

Asset Based Methods. This is obvious. A business is worth the value of its assets. Of course, determining that value is not always easy. Assets have many different values depending upon your perspective. Assets have book value, original cost value, liquidation value, replacement cost value, fair market value and others. Assets being used in a profitable business will have greater value than assets being used in a losing business. So even when using an asset-based approach to value there is still a lot of interpretive work to be done.

Capitalization of Earnings Method. The basic approach is to take historical earnings (usually pre-tax income) and "normalize" for various items, including economic depreciation, owner's salaries, unusual expenses etc. The "normalized" earnings are than capitalized (divided) by a rate that reflects the risk/reward relationship we discussed in previous sessions. The mechanics are easy. The hard part is to come up with the normalized earnings, which are to say what the business will earn in the future, and an appropriate cap rate. If the pieces are correct than the end result will be accurate. If the pieces are incorrect than the end result will be garbage.

Multiple of Discretionary Earnings Method. This is also the

Owner's Discretionary Cash Flow (ODCF) method. In many ways this may be the most logical method to use for small businesses. Ease of calculation is one; but the primary reason is that there is market-based data available to use in this calculation. These comps can provide a generally missing element in valuating small businesses. What did a real buyer pay a real seller for a similar business? With real data, much like what is available to the real estate community, the process of valuing a small business becomes much more market driven and less driven by bias and interpretation of valuators. There are two widely available databases currently available where you can secure this information, BIZCOMPS and Pratt's Stats. A buyer or seller of a small business would be well served to investigate these two resources.

Rules of Thumb. Rules of Thumb take all of the confusing jargon and mathematics loved so much by professional valuators and turns it into an industry specific simple formula. Such as an Accounting Practice will sell for 90% to 150% of annual billings plus fixed assets, an auto repair shop would sell for 3 times monthly gross sales plus inventory, a coin-operated car wash would sell for $10,000 per stall, a restaurant would be 2 times SDC (sellers discretionary cashflow), or a truck stop would be 2-3 times SDC. As you can see these are general statements based on averages—that does not mean they are wrong. On the contrary, you should know the rule of thumb for your industry or the type of business you are considering buying.

There are lots of weaknesses hidden in those simple rule of thumb methods and a person should be very careful about relying only on this one approach. But as an industry benchmark this information is helpful and should be known to every businessperson.

There are numerous books you can use to research your industries rule of thumb. Keep in mind that these rules of thumb are only guidelines and good data to have, not the absolute answers some business owners think they are.

Excess Earnings Method. The basic assumption underlying the Excess Earnings Method is that business profit in excess of a "normal" rate of return on tangible assets is produced by intangible assets. These "excess earnings" can be capitalized into intangible value or goodwill. The steps for applying the method would be:

1. Determine the value of the tangible operating assets and liabilities.
2. Determine the "representative" operating profit.
3. Determine the required rates of return for the tangible operating assets. These rates are used to calculate a return on tangible assets component, which is subtracted from the representative operating profit to derive "excess earnings."
4. Determine the required rate of return for the intangible assets. This rate is used to calculate intangible asset value, or "goodwill." The total business value can then be found by combining the value of the goodwill with the net tangible asset value determined in Step 1.

The capitalization rates used as examples in the rulings were 15 to 20 percent. It has been suggested that the cap rates should range from 20 to 100 percent. We will go into cap rates in greater depth in course eight.

Because this method is widely used, supported by IRS rulings and appears to the average person to be complicated the answer may have more credibility. The weakness with this method is the same as the others in that you have to make certain determinations. How do you define "representative" operating profit? How do you determine a required rate of return on tangible assets? What is required rate of return for intangible assets?

Discounted Future Earnings Method. In theory this is the only method that fully recognizes the elements that create value. We have mentioned several times that the value of a business is its ability to generate a benefit to its owner in the future. Well, if you are talking about the future than you should estimate what the future will be. This method requires the valuator to estimate the future performance of the business. A discount rate is then used to bring those estimated future benefits back to their present value. The discount rate incorporates the same risk/reward relationship as the capitalization rate.

This is the method that theoretically addresses how you should calculate the value of a business. But for small businesses it is not used that often. Why? Probably this is a risk/reward situation in itself. Projecting the future performance of a company with details like sales and profits creates a lot more risk of the valuator being wrong than projecting the future with the use of esoteric capitalization rates. As a professional valuator if I give you a report that shows slow growth for the next 5 years, while you believe there will be very rapid growth, you may question my conclusions regarding value. You can understand the relationship slow future growth verses rapid growth would have on the company value. If I give you a report that has a relatively high cap rate, this may not have much meaning to you as it relates to value. The other reason is cost. A business valuation that incorporates future financial projections will take more time to complete and will cost more.

Course Eight
Capitalization and Discount Rates

The Capitalization Rate (cap rate) is a calculated number that is used as a divisor (or a multiplier), which when applied to an income stream, will provide a present value for that income stream. The cap rate must reflect the current market conditions and the risk/reward aspect of that business. Professional valuators spend a great deal of time developing and defending cap rates. That is because the use of these cap rates will have a tremendous impact on the value of a business.

Cap rates for small closely held business could range from 15 to over 50. That is a tremendous spread, which creates the concern about cap rates. After spending a great deal of time analyzing the financial data from a business and adjusting or recasting the numbers to arrive at "normalized" earnings, using an inappropriate cap rate makes it pointless. If two valuators came up with the same normalized earnings of $100,000 for a business, but one used a cap rate of 20 and one used a cap rate of 30 the resulting values would be $500,000 and $330,000. The same $100,000 in normalized earnings results in values that far apart; due to the cap rate.

Now the big problem. The only way to substantiate cap or discount rates is with market driven data. And that information is very difficult to develop for privately held companies. As a result, a lot of the data comes from the public sector and then is interpreted to fit the private company market. In other words, it is based on the judgment of the valuator. As a result, you can get significant swings in value from on valuator to another based on their interpretation of subjective data.

These rates are often developed using a method called the

"Build-Up Method". This basically involves adding "amounts" to the risk-free rate for areas critical to business success. An example might be:

6.0 Risk Free Rate
2.0 Management
3.0 Competition
4.0 Industry
4.0 Facilities
2.0 Marketing
21.0 Total

There is still a significant aspect of arbitrariness to this whole process. Some valuators use much more arcane approaches and try to justify their results as being more objective. But unless you had a large pool of similar company market driven data to work with developing these numbers will still have a great of judgment built in.

As a small businessperson all of this may seem completely pointless. Except to be able to understand the basis of valuing a business it is important to understand these mechanics. Remember the cap or discount rate is just a way of measuring risk. The risk of achieving particular results in the future.

This concept of future value is well represented by the discounted future earnings method of calculating value. This method projects the earnings of a business into the future. Many valuators dislike this method because it involves actually forecasting the performance of a business in some detail (which at the very least can be very embarrassing if you are dramatically wrong). But with this method you forecast future results and then bring to values back to a "present value" utilizing a discount rate. As I mentioned in some of our first sessions this is the method that clearly follows the logic of what the value of a business really is—the future reward discounted for the risk of achieving that reward.

This session will be short, because the discussion of cap and discount rates is inherently boring. But it is helpful to understand the concepts and to become familiar with the terms.

Course Nine
Sample Valuations

We have covered a lot of ground during this series. We have seen that valuations can be very simple and very complicated. The end result from the simple approach may be as accurate as the end result of the complicated (many method) approach.

In all valuations there is an element of judgment. This is reflected in the projections of future earnings, or the use of discount or capitalization rates to turn historical numbers into a value. Or it may be reflected in the selection of earnings or the adjustments made to earnings. Never let someone suggest to you that there is an absolute right or wrong answer to the valuation question. There are, however, good valuation practices and bad practices.

So even though there is some subjective aspect to every valuation, you should be able to support your opinion of value based on facts. These facts should be submitted along with the statement of value so a reader can interpret whether they agree with your judgments. If you are paying someone to prepare a valuation of your business, you should expect to receive a written report that contains all of the pertinent facts that have been used to arrive at the value conclusion.

For our purposes here we are just going to look at come conclusions and discuss the logic of their valuations. Each sample is a real company.

The first sample is actually 15 companies that I was involved in as a representative of the buyer or seller. These companies were in the outdoor advertising industry (billboards). They were all valued as a multiple of their monthly advertising revenues. This is a rule-of-thumb approach that was exclusively used in the actual transactions of buying/selling these 15 companies.

1. Valuation 36 times monthly advertising revenues.
2. Valuation 48 times monthly advertising revenues.
3. Valuation 60 times monthly advertising revenues.

Those are real world values applied to actual companies that were purchased in 1998 and 1999. The values of 36 times monthly ad revenues were a valuation model that was used for 10 years prior to an aggressive acquisition market developed for these types of companies. But if you went and talked to one of the sellers of these companies about valuations, they would tell you the method they used was X times their monthly revenue. They would have no more paid someone to value their company then they would have burned money. They knew the value.

There were of course underlining investment objectives that were driving this market driven rule-of-thumb. And since there was a very active acquisition market in this industry, this data was the best, most accurate way to value a billboard company.

So, our first sample is simple, straightforward and can be documented on the back of a napkin. But it would be right. Because it is based on what is happening in the marketplace within a particular industry.

It also should be noted that many bad deals were made in this industry because there was too much reliance upon this simple income-based analysis. Often higher than normal expenses would be discovered which would create an entirely different profit potential.

Here is another real-world example. This company had a professional valuation done on their business. The valuator looked at all appropriate methods to establish value. The conclusions were then presented in a methods summary and using a weighting average a value conclusion derived.

Weighted Average of ABC, Inc.

Methodology	Value	Weight	Value
Sales multiple	$4.84M	20%	$0.97M
Cash Flow EBITDA	$4.20M	20%	$0.84M
P/E multiple	$6.83M	20%	$1.37M
Discounted cash flow	$9.80M	20%	$1.96M
Replacement value	$4.50M	20%	$0.90M
			$6.04M

The most interesting thing to note is that using various methods will result in a range of values. In this case $4.2 million to $9.8 million. This range is not uncommon. Averaging these amounts or in this case using a weighting (although each was weighted equally) may not be an accurate approach to value. My personal preference is for the valuator to select the method that is the most accurate for that situation and support that conclusion (although I have used this averaging approach).

A report that states the conclusion of the valuation needs to also state what is being valued and for what purpose. Most typically a valuation is for Fair Market Value, which is the amount expressed in terms of money that may reasonably be expected for property to exchange between a willing buyer and a willing seller with neither being under a compulsion to buy or sell and both fully aware of all relevant facts.

The purpose of the valuation can have impact on the value conclusions. So, the purpose and exactly what is being valued should be clearly stated along with the date the property (business) is being valued.

Another real-world example of valuations is multiples. Often transactions are conducted based upon certain multiples of earnings. This could be earnings before taxes and interest (EBIT) or earnings before taxes, interest, depreciation and amortization (EBITDA). These multiples are once again a shorthand way of conveying certain investment objectives. A multiple of EBITDA of 5 in a certain industry may be the calculation to achieve a 20% return on the investment (if all other factors are "normal"). Multiples will be the shorthand way of discussing value for even large transactions.

So, we can see that the real-world examples can be quite different than the theory. But the underlining principles are still at work—no matter how you say it.

Course Ten
Conclusion

Hopefully you have a better idea of what professional valuators look at to place a value on a small privately held business. As we said in lesson one: the value of any business is actually a very simple concept. But while simple in theory it is often difficult to actually determine. Value is based on the ability of a business to generate a stream of funds into the future. Or in other words how profitable will this business be in the years ahead.

As we have discussed the ability to determine what a business will do in the future involves making various judgments about the quality of the business, the stability of the industry and numerous factors related to the overall economy and the individual business. All very difficult.

We have seen how the risk associated with the business can have a tremendous impact on value. Also, how cap rates and discount rates can modify value to reflect the risk of the business and the uncertainty of the future.

These elements come together in the simplistic way in the form of rules-of-thumbs and multiples. Also, we discussed how much of valuation is intuitive. A business buyer may "feel" good about a business and pay a higher price because of non-financial factors such as good housekeeping. Or a business buyer may walk away from a business that has good numbers but doesn't "feel right". While these aspects are difficult to identify in a tangible way, they are still important elements of value.

If you own a business and someday want to sell you should be aware of all of the aspects that help create value. Much of this is of course financial but there are other elements.

We have discussed several valuation methods and how they are computed. We have also briefly discussed what you should expect from a valuation if you were paying an independent valuator.

Our main purpose with this Course is to acquaint you the business owner or possible business buyer with the theory that creates value in a business. How this is applied can be very different from one set of circumstance to another. But if you can understand what creates value you will have a much better understanding of how to sell your business for the highest price or purchase a business at the least value but still retaining the value in the business.

Appendix
Sample Nondisclosure Agreement

Nondisclosure Agreement

This Mutual Nondisclosure Agreement ("Agreement") is made and entered into as of _____ (*date*) between

_____ (*buyer*) and

_____ *(seller)* (collectively "the parties")

Purpose. The parties wish to explore a business opportunity of mutual interest and in connection with this opportunity, each party may disclose to the other certain confidential technical and business information that the disclosing party desires the receiving party to treat as confidential.

"Confidential Information" means any information disclosed by either party to the other party, directly or indirectly, in writing, orally, or by inspection of tangible objects (including, but not limited to technology, products, business plans, business opportunities, finances, research, development, "know-how," engineering and other designs, architecture, technical data, personnel, and third-Party confidential information), which is designated as "Confidential," "Proprietary," or some similar designation. Information communicated orally will be considered Confidential Information if the information is confirmed in writing as being Confidential Information within a reasonable time after the initial disclosure. Confidential Information may also include information disclosed to the disclosing party by third parties. Confidential Information will not, however, include any information that: (i) was publicly known and made generally available in the public domain prior to the time of disclosure by the disclosing party; (ii) becomes publicly known and made generally available after disclosure by the disclosing party to the receiving party through no action or inaction of the receiving party; (iii) is already in the possession of the receiving party at the time of disclosure by the disclosing party, as shown by the receiving party's files and records; (iv) is obtained by the receiving party from a third party without a breach of the third party's obligations of confidentiality; or (v) is independently developed by the receiving party without use of or reference to the disclosing party's Confidential Information, as shown by documents and other competent evidence in the receiving party's possession.

Non-use and Nondisclosure. Each party will not use the other party's Confidential Information for any purpose except to evaluate and engage in discussions concerning a potential business relationship between the parties. Each party will not disclose the other party's Confidential Information to third parties or to such party's employees, except to those employees of the receiving party who are required to have the information in order to evaluate or engage in discussions concerning the contemplated business relationship. A party may disclose the other party's Confidential Information if required by law so long as the receiving party gives the disclosing party prompt written notice of the requirement prior to the disclosure and assistance in obtaining an order protecting the information from public disclosure. Neither party will reverse engineer, disassemble, or decompile any prototypes, software, or other tangible objects that embody the other party's Confidential Information and that are provided to the party in accordance with this Agreement.

Maintenance of Confidentiality. Each party will take reasonable measures to protect the secrecy of and avoid disclosure and unauthorized use of the other party's Confidential Information. Without limiting the foregoing, each party will take at least those measures that it takes to protect its own most highly confidential information and, prior to any disclosure of the other party's Confidential Information to its employees, will have the employees sign a non-use and nondisclosure agreement that is substantially similar in content to this Agreement. Neither party will make any copies of the other party's Confidential Information unless approved in writing by the other party. Each party will reproduce the other party's proprietary rights notices on any approved copies.

No Obligation. Nothing in this Agreement will obligate either party to proceed with any transaction between them, and each party reserves the right, in its sole discretion, to terminate the discussions contemplated by this Agreement.

No Warranty. ALL CONFIDENTIAL INFORMATION IS PROVIDED "AS IS." NEITHER PARTY MAKES ANY WARRANTIES, EXPRESS, IMPLIED, OR OTHERWISE, REGARDING THE ACCURACY, COMPLETENESS, OR PERFORMANCE OF ITS CONFIDENTIAL INFORMATION.

Return of Materials. All documents and other tangible objects containing or representing Confidential Information and all copies of them will be and remain the property of the disclosing party. Upon the disclosing party's request, the receiving party will promptly deliver to the disclosing party all Confidential Information, without retaining any copies.

No License. Nothing in this Agreement is intended to grant any rights to either party under any patent, copyright, or other intellectual property right of the other party, nor will this Agreement grant any party any rights in or to the Confidential Information of the other party, except as expressly set forth in this Agreement.

Term. The obligations of each receiving party under this Agreement will survive until all Confidential Information of the other party becomes publicly known and made generally available through no action or inaction of the receiving party.

Remedies. Each party acknowledges that any violation or threatened violation of this Agreement may cause irreparable injury to the other party, entitling the other party to seek injunctive relief in addition to all legal remedies.

Miscellaneous. This Agreement will bind and inure to the benefit of the parties and their successors and assigns. This Agreement will be governed by the laws of the state of Washington, without reference to conflict of laws principles. This document contains the entire agreement between the parties with respect to the subject matter of this Agreement. Neither party will have any obligation, express or implied by law, with respect to trade secret or proprietary information of the other party except as set forth in this Agreement. Any failure to enforce any provision of this Agreement will not constitute a waiver of that provision or of any other provision. This Agreement may not be amended, nor any obligation waived, except by a writing signed by both parties. This Agreement may be executed in two or more counterparts, each of which is deemed to be an original, but all of which constitute the same agreement.

Appendix

Sample Due Diligence List for Stock Transaction

A. Organizational Structure:

1. Certificates of Incorporation, Articles of Incorporation, Bylaws, and Charters of the Company and its subsidiaries (or other organizational documents) and all amendments (including Certificates of Designation) thereto and restatements thereof.

2. List of majority-owned subsidiaries directly or indirectly owned by the Company, if any.

3. An organization chart showing the structure of the Company, including a description of ownership and control relationship between the Company and any other person.

4. State of Incorporation.

5. List of directors and officers of the Company and its subsidiaries.

6. List of jurisdictions where the Company and each of its subsidiaries is qualified, licensed or admitted to do business as a foreign corporation, or has offices or facilities, owns or leases property or conducts business.

7. A current listing of operating centers, areas served and territory map.

8. Shareholder and director minutes, ledgers or other records of the Company and its subsidiaries, including

minutes of executive, audit and other committees (board and non-board).

9. Partnerships, Joint Ventures, Affiliate Relationships, Etc.

10. Partnerships, joint ventures and other business enterprises in which the Company or any of its subsidiaries have an interest (debt or equity) and shareholders' or similar agreements to which the Company or any of its subsidiaries is a party, or to which any of the equity holders of the Company or any of its subsidiaries is a party.

11. Agreements by which the Company is subject to any obligation to provide funds or to make any investments in any other entity.

12. Description of affiliate company transactions including terms, transfer pricing, and services provided.

13. Interview key personnel.

14. Employee stock ownership, stock option, stock bonus, stock purchase, stock appreciation, phantom stock or other equity-based plans or agreements or warrants or convertible or exchangeable securities to issue equity interests in the Company or any of its subsidiaries.

B. Capitalization and Equity Holders:

1. List of equity holders and equity ownership of the Company and its subsidiaries, and copies of all business plans and private placement memoranda prepared or used by the Company in connection with securities offerings during the past three years.

2. Copies of filings with SEC and state blue sky authorities and/or evidence of compliance with federal and state securities laws.

3. Trust Agreements or other documents if equity securities are held in a fiduciary capacity or through a voting trust.
4. Agreements granting pre-emptive rights.

C. Financial Statements and Related Matters:

1. Audited consolidated financial statements for the Company and any unconsolidated subsidiaries for the last five years.
2. Unaudited quarterly/monthly financial statements by region or profit center for last two years and most recent interim period.
3. Summary of Company accounting policies including revenue recognition, depreciation/amortization and damage accrual policies.
4. Auditors' letters to management for the prior five years, if any.
5. Schedule of bad debts and agreements with customers or others that might reasonably be expected to result in a loss.
6. Auditors' inquiry letters and replies for the most recent audit.
7. Any reports to the Board of Directors reflecting upon internal corporate controls.
8. Any lawyer responses to Auditor inquiries for the most recent audit.
9. Due diligence reports, consultant studies, or other documents prepared for or by current or prospective investors and/or lenders
10. Monthly DSO reports for last three years.
11. Latest accounts receivable aging report including a com-

parison of the aging of accounts receivable for the last two years and most recent interim period with explanations of any significant changes.

12. General ledger trial balances (in summary form) as of most recent year end and most recent interim period.

13. Detailed schedules of unbilled services in excess of related billings (WIP) as of most recent year end and for the recent interim period with explanations of any potential losses in the WIP accounts.

14. All legal bills for the past 24 months.

15. Listing of cash disbursements for the latest full month.

16. Listing of all inventories.

17. List of other assets.

18. List of all employee advances or loans.

19. Comparative detail of selling, general and administrative expenses for last two years and most recent interim period.

20. Summary of corporate overhead allocation methodology (to location, office or other reporting center).

21. Listing of non-recurring income statement items, if any, for the most recent interim period and any prior period adjustments.

22. Listing of related parties and summaries of transactions with related parties during last two years, and most recent interim period.

23. Detailed breakdown of accrued liabilities account as of most recent year end and latest interim financial statement date

24. Listing of all customer contracts ranked by: sales with cost and gross margin as of most recent year end and next fiscal year (Forecasted).

25. Bridge revenue by customer from most recent year end results to next fiscal year. Include both customer wins and lost customers. In the case of customer wins, please name the previous contractor. In the case of lost customers, please name the new contractor.

26. Contact information for all customers and other customer references, including contact person for damage claim resolution

27. Listing of current operating and capital leases including a schedule of all vehicles and other equipment showing age, cost, method of depreciation/amortization, interest, other fees and current buy out.

28. Listing of fixed assets as of most recent year end and most recent interim period including age, location, cost, current book value and method of depreciation.

29. Listing of capital expenditures for last two years and most recent interim period.

30. Aged accounts payable trial balance for latest interim period.

31. Schedule of loans payable and credit facilities including amounts outstanding, interest rates, commitment fees and minimum payments. Also include the respective lender statements

32. Comparative schedule of accruals and other liabilities as of most recent year end and latest interim period. Include supporting documentation for all balances over $25,000.

33. Reserve analysis for last three years and most recent interim date, including management's reserve methodology for workers' compensation, auto liability and general liability.

34. Workers' compensation, auto liability and general liability

claim history for the most recent 4 years.

D. Tax Matters:

1. Copies of all returns for latest closed and all open years for the Company and its subsidiaries—including income, sales and use, real property, capital gains, franchise and others.
2. Audit and revenue agents' reports.
3. Settlement documents and correspondence for last five years.
4. Agreements waiving statute of limitations or extending time.
5. Tax sharing arrangements and tax indemnity agreements to which the Company or any of its subsidiaries is a party.
6. Schedule of any plans or arrangements that could trigger issues under Section 280G (excess parachute payments), or other plans or arrangements that could result in payments or benefits as a result of the transaction contemplated with Asplundh Tree Expert Co.
7. Copies of accountants' due diligence reports, for example:
   a. Fair market value and asset bases of assets of the Company and its subsidiaries, including the respective basis of each parent corporation in the stock of its subsidiaries
   b. Summary of timing differences between book and tax accounting methods for the past five years and for the short year of acquisition
   c. Summary of significant tax accounting method elections made within the past ten years
   d. Summary of available carryovers (e.g., net operating

loss, investment credit, foreign tax credit) and the expiration dates for each carryover

8. S-Corp
   a. Copy of Form 2553. It should be marked "RECEIVED" by the IRS.
   b. Acknowledgement letter from the IRS stating the company is an S-Corp.
   c. Tax year if presently other than a calendar year.
   d. Was there a prior election and revocation and then a new election?
   e. Shareholder listing on the Form 2553.

E. Employees, Benefit Plans and Labor Matters:

1. A list of all employees of the company and each subsidiary. Indicate age, sex, years of service, function, location, annual compensation, rate of pay, salary or non-salary, full-time or part-time, temporary employee, whether or not member of collective bargaining unit, provide amounts relating to base pay, bonuses, and other compensation.
2. Union and collective bargaining agreements, if any.
3. Organization charts—Corporation and Field Operations
4. All agreements or arrangements (and a description of each oral agreement or arrangement) between the company or any subsidiary and any present or former director, officer, employee, or agent with respect to length, duration, or conditions of employment (or termination of employment), salaries, bonuses, percentage compensation, deferred compensation, or any other form or remuneration.
5. For each qualified pension, retirement, savings and prof-

it-sharing plans currently in effect, please provide a plan description, sample summary annual reports and other materials required to be furnished to employees with respect to benefit plans and the benefit cost per plan.

6. For each health, life, disability, accident and other welfare benefit plans currently in effect, please provide a plan description, sample summary annual reports and other materials required to be furnished to employees with respect to benefit plans and the benefit cost per plan.

7. For each non-qualified retirement, bonus, incentive and deferred compensation plans or programs currently in effect, please provide a plan description, sample summary annual reports and other materials required to be furnished to employees with respect to benefit plans and the benefit cost per plan

8. Trust or other funding agreements, including insurance contracts, service provider agreements and agreements with investment managers, for benefit plans.

9. Forms 5500 (or the equivalent thereof), including schedules, and actuarial reports for the most recent three years.

10. Most recent accountings for benefits plans funded through a trust.

11. For each defined benefit plan, a statement of plan assets and liabilities based on plan assumptions and assumptions prescribed by the Pension Benefit Guaranty Corporation.

12. Estimate of potential withdrawal liability from each multi-employer plan.

13. Severance and separation, fringe benefit and perquisite, holiday, vacation, leave of absence, layoff, day and dependent care, legal services and cafeteria plans, policies and agreements.

14. Employee policy manuals and/or handbooks, supervisor's guides, and general personnel policies and procedures manuals and/or handbooks relating to the company or any subsidiary and copies of any other documents setting forth employment policies for the past 4 years.

15. Summaries of labor disputes, strikes, work stoppages, organizational efforts or other union action or concerted action by employees within the last five years, grievance proceedings, arbitration or requests for arbitration or labor regulatory body charges or complaints; and summary of employment-related claims by employees or former employees of the Company or any of its subsidiaries within the last years, where the claims were in the nature of wrongful termination, discrimination, harassment or the like

16. Current compensation information (including base salary, bonus, options, etc.) for all exempt (or non-hourly) employees.

17. Facility listing showing number of employees by facility, indicate unions.

18. All consulting agreements and other agreements (and a description of each oral agreement) with independent contractors, to which the company or subsidiary is a part.

19. Has the company or any subsidiary been subject of any union organization attempt within the last 4 years, or is the company or any subsidiary currently the subject of any union campaign?

20. Has the company or any subsidiary been the subject of any charges, investigation, or order under any law relating to labor standards (including minimum wage, over-time pay, occupational safety and health) or any law regulat-

ing employment during the last three years? If so, please provide copies of pertinent documents.

21. Has there been any litigation pending or threatened between the company or any subsidiary and any government agency on behalf of any present or former employee, or applicant for employment, in the last 4 years? If so, please describe and provide copies of all related documentation.

22. Have any charges been filed or threatened against the company or any subsidiary with the NLRB or any state or local relations authority within the last 4 years? If so, please provide copies of pertinent documents.

23. Has any present or former employee filed or threatened any charges within the last 4 years claiming that the company or any subsidiary unlawfully discriminated on the basis of race, age, sex or concerning any employee relations claims including sexual or any other form of harassment or failure to pay wages or commissions under state or federal law? If so, provide copies of pertinent documents.

24. Copy of Shop Rules

25. Copies of any grievance settlements or arbitration awards.

26. Workers comp premium rate and unemployment tax rates and premiums paid in the last 3 years. Most current SUTA reports.

27. Description of all compensation plans including bonuses, incentives, commissions and transportation benefits.

28. Summary of vacation/leave accrual policy and description of accrual process with most recent valuations (accrued hours/dollars).

29. Names of 3rd party providers of payroll and other HR services including a brief description of services offered

and fee structure.

F. Other Contracts and Arrangements of the Company and its Subsidiaries

Whether written or oral (in which case, reasonable summaries thereof) including all amendments and waivers:

1. Loan and credit agreements, note purchase agreements, agreements and letters affirming bank lines of credit, indentures, promissory notes and other evidence of in-debtedness and compensating balance arrangements, including copies of all instruments and agreements creating security interests in assets, UCC-1 filings, etc.
2. List of known contingent liabilities and obligations.
3. Guarantees and related agreements.
4. Copies of vendor and customer contracts representing costs or revenues of over $10,000 for most recent year end and current.
5. Contracts or other arrangements with affiliates and associates, including all directors, officers and key employees and their families and affiliated or related persons.
6. Non-compete agreements or agreements restricting lines of business.
7. Documentation relating to mergers, consolidations and acquisitions and dispositions of businesses or significant amounts of assets in the last five years.
8. Sale and leaseback arrangements.
9. Powers of attorney and similar delegations of authority.
10. Brokers' or finders' agreements currently in effect, if any, and, whether or not in effect, that could result in a payment or benefit being owed to any party as a result of the

contemplated transaction with ATE.

11. A schedule of consents that would be required for the consummation of the proposed transaction under all material contracts and agreements.

12. All other material contracts and agreements of the Company, including contracts outside the ordinary course of business, not otherwise covered by this request.

G. Licenses/Permits:

1. Material license agreements running to and from the Company or a subsidiary (including environmental licenses),

2. Material permits or government consents running to the Company or a subsidiary.

H. Insurance of the Company and its Subsidiaries:

1. Identification of current Commercial broker of record and for the past three years.

2. List of all insurance contracts, including D&O, equipment, crime, umbrellas, surety, workers' compensation, auto liability, property, damage, and other liability insurance along with a summary of key insurance terms (e.g., premiums, exposure limits, deductibles, underwriter, renewal dates, etc.).

3. Current EMR rating for workers compensation and for past five years.

4. Summary of key man insurance in place.

5. Notices from carriers denying liability or coverage or

asserting reservation of rights under existing policies or adequacy of insurance coverage.

6. Summary of experience in self-insurance programs, if any.
7. A summary of workers compensation claims experience for the company and each subsidiary for the last 5 years.
8. A summary of claims experience for the company under all insurance policies (property, general liability and auto).
9. Copies of actuarial reports or studies done on workman's comp, auto and general liability claims.
10. A schedule of insurance reserves relating to the company and any subsidiary.

I. Litigation and Regulatory Matters:

1. Litigation list (including pending and threatened matters), together with letters to auditors with respect to litigation the last three years.
2. List of governmental and administrative proceedings and investigations (including pending and threatened matters and including in connection with environmental matters and employment related proceedings).
3. Consent decrees and injunctions, judgments, orders, settlement agreements, etc.

J. Intellectual Property of the Company and its Subsidiaries:

1. List of service markets, service names, trademarks and trade names, patents, copyrights, and other intellectual property rights.
2. List of computer programs and related documentation.

3. Registrations and applications for any of the foregoing.
4. Consulting agreements relating to the creation of intellectual property by independent contractors.

K. Information Technology:

1. Outline of the Company's computerized information systems, including summary descriptions of the Company's ticket management system, fieldwork management systems, billing systems, and financial/accounting systems.
2. Listing of IT projects (productivity improvement initiatives, field automation initiatives, financial systems, etc.)
3. Listing of all software licenses at most recent year end and most recent interim period.
4. Connectivity diagram of IT infrastructure.

L. Documents Related to Real or Personal Property:

1. A schedule of all material deeds, mortgages, title reports and policies and all leases and related agreements concerning all real property owned or occupied by the Company.
2. A schedule of all material agreements encumbering real or personal property of the Company, including mortgages, liens, deeds of trust and security agreements.
3. A listing of vehicles and equipment including make, model, age, location, condition, mileage, replacement schedule and owned vs. leased. (See Attached Schedule to complete)
4. Detailed listing of field-deployed laptop computers.

5. Detailed listing and service providers for field-deployed cellphones, or equivalent.
6. Detailed listing and service providers for back-office land lines (long distance and 800 toll-free numbers) and data lines.
7. A schedule of all significant leases of real property and all leases of items of personal property having a value at the time of acquisition of $50,000 or more and used by the Company as either lessor or lessee, showing annual rent (or the method of computation thereof) and the expiration date.
8. All material warranty and service agreements to which the Company is a party.
9. All title insurance policies for material properties owned or leased by the Company.

M. Environmental Documents:

1. All notices to or from environmental regulatory authorities, including but not limited to inspection and monitoring reports, notices of violation, noncompliance or future inspection, regarding air pollution or emission controls, waste disposal, surface or wastewater discharge, maintenance or registration of aboveground or underground storage tanks, septic systems or any activities of the Company.
2. All environment-related memoranda, audits or inspection reports, whether created by the Company, its agents or employees or by the third party.
3. All documents relating to the presence, removal, abatement or remediation of asbestos or asbestos-containing

material on or from the Company's property.

4. All environment-related insurance policies, notices or claims for coverage, responses to any such notices or claims and related analyses or memoranda of the Company or its insurance brokers or agents.

5. All documents relating to environmental liabilities affecting the Company or its operations arising from any acquisition or sales by the Company of any asset or business.

6. All environmental impact reports or statements, including all public notices and comments, prepared in connection with the construction or modification of any of the Company's facilities.

N. Operational Information:

1. Performance data by operating center and Company roll-up for last 3 years including:
   a. Safety—incident, frequency and severity statistics for vehicle and workers comp.
   b. Productivity:
      i. Number of billable units per man-hour.
      ii. Overtime hours as a % of base paid.
   c. Summary of Customer-Performed Quality Audits performed broken down by customer.

Stay in Touch

Stay in touch with Ted Clifton and Success Paths business books. Clifton's background is financial (CPA, Controller, CFO) with over 30 years of real-world experience as a financial advisor, business owner of fifteen business ventures and as a business broker with valuation experience.

Learn more about successful business practices and small business matters, such as selling or buying a business, starting and running a small business and how to value a small business.

Newsletters are free and informative. Opt-out at any time. Thanks for your interest in Success Paths Business Books.

Subscribe today at:
https://mailchi.mp/1e966d569a72/success-paths

Ted Clifton Mystery Books

Business books and mystery books might be an odd combination, but maybe they are connected in a mysterious way—if you enjoy mysteries, check out these offerings from Ted Clifton. Learn more at www.tedclifton.com.

Pacheco & Chino Mysteries—A retired sheriff, an enigmatic bait-shop owner, and an Apache fishing guide team up to solve a mystery that starts with an out-of-place show dog—and ends much deadlier.

The Bootlegger's Legacy—Joe and Mike, middle-aged losers, have uncovered a promise of abundant riches—if only they can solve the clues left behind by Mike's bootlegger dad.

Vincent Malone—Disgraced investigator and alcoholic Vincent Malone finds new life as a shuttle driver for a B&B—then a guest is murdered and his investigative skills are suddenly front-and-centre again.

The Muckraker Series—New journalism grad Tommy Jacks hires on as a political reporter with a struggling paper, but is quickly pulled into an ugly newspaper war when a rival reporter is murdered.

Doctor Hightower—Ted Clifton's new Mystery/Sci-Fi serial, available on Amazon Vella soon!

Ted Clifton Series Starter Set—Amazon ebook containing the complete first books of the Pacheco & Chino, Vincent Malone, and Muckraker mystery series.

Have questions or comments for Ted Clifton? He can be reached at ask@tedclifton.com.

Thanks for being a reader!

CPSIA information can be obtained
at www.ICGtesting.com
Printed in the USA
BVHW041705160523
664273BV00004B/236

9 781773 421131